ENJOY YOUR KIDS
ENJOY YOUR WORK

Also by Joan Sturkie

CHRISTIAN PEER COUNSELING: LOVE IN ACTION

LISTENING WITH LOVE

A PEER COUNSELOR'S POCKET BOOK

ACTING IT OUT

ENJOY YOUR KIDS
ENJOY YOUR WORK

JOAN STURKIE

WORD PUBLISHING
Dallas · London · Vancouver · Melbourne

Enjoy Your Kids, Enjoy Your Work

Copyright © 1991 by Joan Sturkie

All rights reserved. No portion of this book may be reproduced in any form, except for brief quotations in reviews, without written permission from the publisher.

Unless otherwise indicated, Scripture quotations used in this book are from The Everyday Bible, New Century Version, copyright © 1987, 1988 by Word Publishing, Dallas, Texas 75039. Used by permission. Those identified KJV are from the King James Version.

Library of Congress Cataloging-in-Publication Data

Sturkie, Joan, 1932–
    Enjoy your kids, enjoy your work : a working mother's guide to leading a double life / by Joan Sturkie.
    p. cm.
  ISBN 0-8499-3210-6
    1. Working mothers—United States. 2. Parenting—United States. 3. Motherhood—Religious aspects—Christianity. I. Title.
HQ759.48.S78   1991
306.874'3—dc20   90-48386
                                                                        CIP

Printed in the United States of America

12349 AGF 987654321

To the memory of my mother, *Annie Louise (Lola) Whisenhunt* (1898–1957), who watchfully cared for her only child with unconditional love and unrelenting patience, yet who willingly gave that child permission to make her own decisions and embrace life to the fullest.

and

To the memory of *Ruth (Gunny) Gunderson* (1900–1982), who entered our home as a part-time baby-sitter for the children, but who soon became an important member of our family. Her love of God and all His creatures great and small was an inspiration to us all.

and

To my husband, *Roy*, and our eight children and one son-in-law, *Alissa, David, Matthew, Kimberly* and *Kyle, Paul, Timothy, John,* and *Elizabeth*, who have made joy a common household word for me.

and

To *James Trenton Hearon*, my first grandchild, who made his appearance while this book was being written and who gave me yet a new joy, that of being a grandmother.

Contents

Foreword ix
Acknowledgments xi
Introduction 1
 1. Identifying with the Status of the Working Mother 6
 2. Meeting Expectations 11
 3. Choosing the Right Job 20
 4. Finding Good Childcare 32
 5. Giving Support to Your Children 42
 6. Having a Supportive Husband 49
 7. Sharing Holidays 58
 8. Being a Single Parent 71
 9. Arranging Private Time for Mom 81
 10. Using "Never" and "Always" 94
 11. Learning to Communicate 111
 12. Having Backup Plans When Everything Is Going Wrong 123
 13. Enjoying Your Children—Enjoying Your Work 130
 14. Enjoying Your Adult Children 140
 15. Hearing from the Mothers 150
 16. Concluding Thoughts 211
Bibliography 215

Foreword

Motherhood used to be the goal of every little baby-doll-carrying girl. She pictured herself as Mrs. Cleaver, happily married in the perfect suburban house with Wally, Beaver, and Mr. Cleaver to care for. But those days are gone, and today's media paint an entirely different picture of motherhood. Too often, having children is seen as a burden, rather than the blessing God intended it to be. Kids are thought to be a stopping place for a woman's education, a stumbling block to her social life, and a sidetrack from her career. As a result, many women today have made a choice to skip the "Mommy Track" altogether and go straight for the top without the impediment of children.

So where does that leave mothers? Many are feeling frustrated in their choices and uncomfortable in playing a game where all the rules have changed. That is why Joan Sturkie's book, *Enjoy Your Kids, Enjoy Your Work*, is so important for today's mothers. Whether your job is outside the home, in the home, or whether your job *is* the home, Joan will help you find balance in your personal and professional life while still keeping your children in the place of importance they need.

In the last decade, many women have found that despite what they have been told, it isn't possible to have it all. In fact a recent *Time* magazine article on the state of women today said that rather than having it all, women have just "had it." They have found that by trying to stretch themselves they have gotten stretched out and stressed out. They have learned that there are things in life that are more important in the long run than breaking the "glass ceiling" on the career ladder.

While Joan leaves you to make your own choice about working outside the home, working in the home, or being a full-time mom, she offers excellent suggestions that come from her own experience as a "working mom," from other mothers who have worked outside the home, and from mothers who have not. In *Enjoy Your Kids, Enjoy Your Work*, Joan encourages mothers to decide for themselves which choice is best for them and their families. Whatever you decide, to have a job in addition to raising your children, or to stick with that one job of being a mom, Joan will help you do both—*Enjoy Your Kids, Enjoy Your Work*.

—Florence Littauer

Acknowledgments

I would like to thank the mothers who shared their philosophies on children, husbands, and work, and gave me permission to use their ideas and suggestions in this book. I hope their wise and helpful words, interspersed throughout these pages, will be a blessing upon the mothers who read them.

Introduction

I enjoy my kids. I enjoy my work. I have for over thirty-one years. Even though my career has changed several times—from registered nurse, to full-time wife and mother, to businesswoman, to high-school counselor, to consultant and author—and my children have grown from infants to adults, I still find work satisfying and challenging, and my children a blessing to enjoy.

"Even when all eight of the children were young and you worked full time?" I'm asked frequently.

"Yes, even then," I reply. With only eleven and a half years between the ages of the oldest child and the youngest, they were all young virtually at the same time. One year, all nine of us left the house every morning to spend our day in the same school district.

It was during those years I worked as a high-school counselor that I found all working women were not enjoying their children. During parent conferences, an all too frequent comment I heard was, "I give up! I don't have time to try to handle John's (or Mary's) problems anymore. Just please take care of it. Whatever you think is best, that's fine with me." What I wanted to say in response to that statement was, "Don't ever give up on your child! No matter how busy you are or how frustrating the problem may be, hang in there." What I would actually say was something a little less direct and somewhat more tactful. My perception was that too many parents (yes, even Christian parents) were feeling overwhelmed, frazzled, and at the end of their ropes. Parenting was not a joyful experience as it should have been. Instead, it was a chore they were anxious to complete.

These feelings are being voiced not only by mothers of teenagers. Some moms are feeling the same way about their preschoolers. Linda, a young working mother of a two-year-old son and a four-year-old daughter, expressed her frustration poignantly when she said, "I just want this time of my life to hurry and pass. Looking forward to the time when the children are grown is what keeps me going from day to day." Working and motherhood seem to be so frustrating and draining to some that survival is their main goal.

How sad! How very sad that mothers (good, well-meaning mothers) like Linda will allow these wonderful years to go by and never discover one of the fruits of the Christian life—joy. They keep waiting, intending to look for it later; but from what I have observed, the longer one waits to find joy, the harder it is to find. It becomes that illusive part of life that is just around the corner, never within reach. Yet we know that Jesus says in John 15:11, "I have told you these things so that you can have the same joy I have. I want your joy to be the fullest joy." That includes mothers, too.

I've written this book for those mothers who want more in life than just survival. I've written it for those who want joy, as a parent and as a worker, whether that work is done at home or in the marketplace. I've not written it to try to convince anyone that she should or should not work outside the home. That decision is yours to make. Some mothers will say, "But it's not a choice. I must work because my paycheck is necessary for us to live." This is certainly true in many homes today, particularly the ones with a single parent.

"Some people say, 'Why bother working, if it takes so much of your salary just to pay for childcare?' I answer by saying, 'But you don't understand. We need what's left over. We can't get by without it.'" —Dawn Brainard

---

Other mothers do have a choice, and they may choose to work for a variety of reasons. Some may want to add income to the family budget to attain a higher lifestyle, such as a larger home, a new car, or a greater social position in the community. Others may want some of the simpler pleasures of life: a family vacation, music lessons for the children, stylish clothing, or evenings out at sporting events or cultural affairs.

Some mothers want to continue the career for which they have prepared themselves through many years of study. A young executive in the business world summed up her feelings by saying, "Staying at home with my one-year-old has never really been an option for me. If I get off my career track, I will not be able to get back on later."

Other professional and nonprofessional mothers have different reasons. One mother expressed her feelings to me in a very straightforward way when she said, "I hate staying at home. I don't like housework. The kids are at school all day, and I'm bored to death. Working gives me the opportunity to hire a cleaning person, enjoy a family dinner at a restaurant once a week, and have money for the extras I wouldn't have if I didn't work." Another mother said, "I like the stimulation of being with other people, even if it does take most of my paycheck to pay for services I could do if I stayed at home."

Mothers who work at home feel just as strongly about their chosen positions. A pediatrician said, "I wouldn't think of missing these early stages with my child. Nothing is more important to me than being at home during these formative years." A former secretary voiced the same feelings, saying, "I work much harder at home than I did in the office. In fact, I am totally exhausted at the end of some days. Even with a more demanding schedule, longer working hours, and no weekends off, I wouldn't change positions with anyone, for any amount of money."

A mother of two young schoolchildren states, "Even with my husband's salary (as a vice-president in an advertising agency) my staying at home means we must make sacrifices. It's hard to live on one salary; but we feel that it is important for me to stay at home until the children have graduated from high school. Teenagers need a mother at home as much as younger children do, maybe more."

> *"The reason that I don't work is to be with my children. When I was young, all my friends played with Barbie dolls, but I always wanted to play with baby dolls. I have always wanted to be a mother, and when I got to be one, I wanted it to be on a full-time basis."* —Vicki Rockett

Whatever your reason is for being employed in the workplace or at home, that work should be enjoyed, because you spend a great portion of your day—and your life—doing it. Being a parent must also be enjoyed because you are a model to your children. One of the best ways to produce happy, well-adjusted children is to exemplify these qualities yourself.

I have written this book to give encouragement and support to the Christian working mother, no matter where she performs her work. The overall purpose is for women to find suggestions and ideas here to apply to their own lives so they may enjoy being mothers during those child-rearing years, and at the same time enjoy their work, whether they are doing it by choice or by necessity.

Some of the material in this book is from my own personal experiences, while some is from the experiences of other mothers. I certainly do not have all the answers, but I have traveled the road. I worked up until the day I delivered my first child, and I returned to full-time work five months later. Frankly, I did not enjoy being away from my baby; but at the time, it was a financial necessity. When the baby was a year old, I was able to stay home full time. Then, from the time my second child was born until the youngest was three years old, I worked only part time. Being a registered nurse, I could work on weekends when my husband was at home with the children.

Some years, I worked only at home. However, most of my friends think of me as a full-time working mother because I resumed my professional career when the eight children were all living at home, with the youngest still being a preschooler. Often when people found out I had eight children and worked, too, they would ask, "How do you do it?" Smiling, I would respond, "With a lot of prayer."

One day a woman said, "That may be true; but you must be doing some other things also to raise eight apparently happy, well-adjusted kids." I've thought about that comment over the years, as I have heard it voiced on other occasions. Now that the last child is away at college, I can look back, probably with a little bit more objectivity, and see what things were done that might be helpful to pass on to others. I won't go into all the things I should have done differently, though. There were certainly many of those! Neither will I hold my children up as model kids, and I'm sure they wouldn't hold me up as a model mother. Either situation would be untrue and embarrassing to all of us. Rather than emphasize my own kids and our lives, I will take the principles I have learned and include the experiences of many other mothers to give this book a broader base. There will be times, of course, when I refer to my own family and the special events in our lives.

I enjoy being a mom. I enjoy my work. Is this possible? Yes, of course. It is not only possible, it is being done every day. How do working parents do it? They learn how. You can too.

1

Identifying with the Status of the Working Mother

If Rip Van Winkle had slept from 1960 until 1990, he would have awakened to find a very different world for women. According to the United States Department of Labor, Bureau of Labor Statistics, 34.8 percent of women worked outside the home in 1960, in contrast to 57.8 percent today. Over the same time span, the number of female doctors climbed from 15,672 to 180,200, the number of women lawyers and judges rose from 7,500 to 180,000, and the number of female engineers increased from 7,404 to 174,000. Currently 68 percent of women with children under age eighteen are in the work force, in contrast to 28 percent of the women with children in 1960.

Women who work today earn only sixty-six cents for each dollar men earn. One reason for this is that 59 percent of employed women work in low-paying jobs—some because such jobs tend to be more compatible with child rearing, and some because they are not trained for higher-level jobs. The wage gap and the lack of affordable childcare have taken their greatest toll on unmarried women, particularly single mothers. Today more than 60 percent of adults below the federal poverty level are women.

Will the trend of women working outside the home continue? Yes, says the United States Bureau of Census. It has predicted that by the year 2000 the portion of women working outside the home will increase to 61.5 percent. In comparison, men in the labor force will decrease from 76 percent to 74.7 percent.

Decisions Center, Inc., a New-York-based marketing-research firm, selected 1,100 women and 1,000 men from 350 college campuses for a new survey. They found that nine out of ten of these young women plan to combine a briefcase with marriage and babies, and the majority of the college men surveyed approve of that decision. "The message to employers is clear: Many college-educated women employees plan to climb the proverbial ladder with children in tow," said Decisions Center's Rick Lund.

Will the increase of women choosing to work signify that more will be enjoying what they are doing? We would hope so; but that may not be true. Many are working now out of necessity, and there is no evidence to support any change in the future. But we must realize that some women have always worked because of necessity and many of them have enjoyed their work.

In the early days of this country, women worked beside their husbands to carve out a place for themselves and their families in their new homeland. They tended farm animals, made cloth and sewed for the family, traded farm produce, and gathered firewood. Until the Industrial Revolution, work performed by mothers was almost always done in their homes or in nearby fields. These mothers watched after their own children or shared the responsibility with an aunt or grandmother living in the home.

The exception to this, of course, was the single mothers, who managed alone to work and provide for their children because, as one mother of four put it, "I had no choice. It was either work or starve. I knew I had to protect my kids, so I worked two jobs every day. My kids are all grown up now, have good jobs, and are responsible members of the community. They learned early that work is honorable, and that a mother works because she loves her children."

"My mother-in-law and I have quite a contrast: She worked when it wasn't popular for mothers to work, and forty years later, I'm staying at home when it isn't popular for mothers to stay home." —VICKI ROCKETT

Around 1970, women entered the workplace in record numbers, with the typical mother leaving home after her youngest child reached the age of twelve. By 1975, that had changed, and the mother waited only until her child entered school. By 1985, the majority were back at work by the time the child was two years old. Today, more than 50 percent of all new mothers go back to work before their child's first birthday. What has caused this change? Some return to work because of financial necessity, while others who postponed having a child until their career was well established now find they can only be away from that work for a short period of time without jeopardizing their jobs.

According to the United States Department of Labor, the age and education of the mother is a factor in the decision she makes concerning working after her child is born. Approximately 68 percent of women who had their first child at age thirty or older continue to work, compared with 54 percent of new mothers age eighteen to twenty-four. In addition, 63 percent of new mothers with college degrees stayed on the job, compared with 38 percent of those who only completed high school.

Ironically, with this new trend to return to work when a baby is very young, the mothers who do stay home until later sometimes feel guilty. One young mother expressed her frustrations by saying, "Last week a neighbor asked me why I hadn't gone back to work. I explained to her that

---
> *"Staying at home is not a popular decision. There is a lot of pressure to continue to work."*
> —JANICE GUTIERREZ
---

in the previous year Jim and I had denied ourselves all luxuries and saved every penny possible so that I could stay at home for a year after Tamera's birth. It was a good decision and I'm very happy being at home; but just the way my neighbor asked the question made me feel guilty. She went back to work when her baby was six weeks old; and after our conversation, I began to wonder if she felt that I didn't quite measure up or that I'm lazy because I'm still home." Another mother complained that she is tired of justifying to her peers why she stays at home. "They just don't seem to understand that I feel very fulfilled. I don't need a career to make my life complete. My husband and baby do that for me," she stated.

While some mothers feel guilty if they stay home, others feel guilty if they work outside the home. The joy of life eludes both. How then can a mother find that joy no matter which lifestyle she has chosen? The first answer to this question is that one will find joy if she feels what she is doing is right. Many women have responded by saying, "I want to do what is right. But how can I know I've made the correct decision?"

In Proverbs 16:1–3, we read, "People make plans in their hearts. But only the Lord can make those plans come true. A person may believe he is doing right. But the Lord will judge his reasons. Depend on the Lord in whatever you do. Then your plans will succeed." So we find the first step to joy is to depend on the Lord.

In Ephesians 3:20, we find, "With God's power working in us, God can do much, much more than anything we can ask or think of." That is the second answer to our question—we find joy because God can make us so much more successful in our work than we can ever make ourselves.

In Ephesians 6:7, we read, "Do your work, and be happy to do it. Work as if you were serving the Lord, not as if you were serving only men." So the third answer to finding joy in our work is to perform our tasks, at home or at the workplace, as a service to God.

"Parents have choices. We may choose joy; we may choose to love. We need to pause before we make choices, and make sure we are choosing the right one." —Virginia Berry Hoffman

---

In making a decision as to how you will relate to the status of women in today's society and how you will find joy in doing it, remember to follow the three steps listed above: Depend on the Lord by giving yourself totally to His will for your life; do all your work as a service to Him; and enjoy the fruits of your labors, knowing that He has given you far greater success than you could have achieved by yourself. Your decision to work at home full time or to be employed in the marketplace will then be the right decision for you.

Remember also your current decision may be right for you only for a given period of time. If you are an at-home mom, you may decide at the time your last child enters school to seek God's will about working outside the home. If you are currently away from home, you may find your financial goals have been accomplished, and you are ready to work full time at home.

Seeking God's will concerning your work status is an ongoing process, and as God gives us life abundantly, He also gives us joyful surprises along the way. Those surprises may involve your work. They may even result in a change of career. Whatever the outcome, you can be assured that you will, "Rejoice in the Lord, you who do right. Praise his holy name" (Ps. 97:12).

2

Meeting Expectations

Susan confided to her friend, "I just can't do it! Too much is expected of me."

"Do you mean too much is expected at work?" Mary asked.

"I mean too much is expected every place: at home, work, the children's school, church."

"By whom?" Mary probed.

"At home, by John, of course," Susan answered, quickly adding, "but a husband has a right to expect certain things of a wife. My father certainly expected my mother to have food on the table for him, his shirts ironed and hanging in the closet, and his socks neatly tucked away in his chest."

"And you want to do the same things for John that your mother did for your father?"

"Yes, of course."

"And the things you do for the children are the same ones your mother did for you?"

"Yes, those things and more. Ben and Molly are involved in more school and church activities than I was."

"Did your mother work outside the home?"

"No, but she worked very hard at home."

"And you want to do the same as she did and work outside your home too?"

"I thought I could do it."

"What about your job? Is your boss real demanding?"

"Mr. Turner? Oh, no, he's very nice; but I have been the top salesperson in the office for the past three months, and I can't let up now. If I continue like this I'll be in line for the free trip to Hawaii next summer."

"And the expectations at Ben and Molly's school?"

"The Parent Teacher Association meets at night because there are so many of us who work. I took the job as president this year because the nominating committee was having a hard time finding someone."

"And the expectations at church?" Mary continued to inquire.

"You know I sing in the choir. I also promised to teach the five-year-olds in Sunday school — but just until they can find someone else."

"You also work in the refreshment stand at the Little League field."

"But that's because I'm Ben's team mother."

"Sounds like you are trying to be a super-mom to me," Mary said frankly.

"No, I don't want to be a super-mom."

"But who is really putting all the expectations on you? Is it John, Ben or Molly, Mr. Turner, the school, the church? Or is it you?"

Fortunately, Susan began to think seriously about that question. It did not take her long to realize that she was partly the cause of her pressures, and that she must be the one to take steps to correct the problem. She spoke to John first and solicited his help. He agreed to share the evening meal preparation with her and to take his shirts to the laundry. At first, Susan felt guilty about not doing everything at home, but soon the sheer pleasure of having a little more time in the evening overshadowed the guilt feelings. She then talked to the children about the school activities they considered most important for her to support. A list was made and priorities given to each activity. She also took a year's leave from singing in the choir at church. This was personally the most difficult change she made, because she found joy in singing, and was reluctant to give it up. Next year she planned to reeevaluate her situation. Maybe at that time she could reinstate choir participation.

"A working woman has to keep her priorities straight. If she ever loses sight of family, a woman has lost it. I don't care how big her business is or how small, if she ever sells out to something besides her family, she's messed up big time." — MARCIE PERRY

In looking at Susan's solution, the question could be asked, "Why didn't she give up one of her less enjoyable duties and remain in the choir?" The answer might be that Susan felt there was no one available to fill the other positions. She was PTA president because no one else would do it, and she was teaching the Sunday school class only until a replacement could be found. Could it be that Susan had not developed sufficient assertive skills to be able to say no?

This is a common problem with generous and kind women who allow other people to "program" them. After all, doesn't Proverb 31:27 say, "She watches over her family. And she is always busy"? And isn't it true that a busy person is the one to ask to do a job because that person can always be counted on to get the work done? While the answer to both of those questions may be yes, one must look a step further and see just how busy one can be without suffering emotionally and physically from a load that may cause too many pressures.

It is commendable to be sacrificing at times and to take the jobs that may be difficult to fill; but before a mother says yes to another commitment, she should remember to do ten things:

1. *Take time before giving your answer.* The decision probably does not have to be made today.

2. *Stand firm, even if you are coerced to give an immediate answer.*

3. *Evaluate how badly you are really needed.* A good salesperson may imply that no one else can do the job except you. While the words sound nice and are quite flattering, they usually aren't true. There are very few jobs which only one person is capable of doing. Of course, there are always exceptions. You may, indeed, be the only piccolo player in your church orchestra!

4. *Ask yourself what your motives are for taking the job. Are you just flattered at being asked?* Do you believe you can really contribute something unique? Do you think it is your duty? Will the consequences to the group or organization be long-lasting if you do not say yes, or will it matter ten years from now if you did or did not fill the position? Do you really want to do it?

5. *List the other options available to the group seeking your services.* While these may not be numerous, there usually are at least a few, if one seriously looks for them.

6. *Look at your present time schedule and see if it will be possible to add anything else.* Be honest with yourself. Being a martyr is not the answer.

7. *Ask yourself how your decision will affect your family.* If it means giving up any time you are presently spending with your family, talk to them before eliminating that time.

8. *Pray about your decision and seek God's will.* Remember situations are never too small to bring before God.

9. *Make your decision, and then stand by it.* Do not succumb to pressure to change your mind.

10. *Be joyful with your decision.* Do not feel guilty, no matter what may happen in the future. You have done what you feel is the right thing to do.

Women with jobs away from home are not the only ones who find that others' expectations of them are too high. The same thing can happen to a woman who stays at home; in fact, it may happen to her more frequently. When a person does not have a position that requires a certain number of hours away from the house, people sometimes think that person has a lot of free time. PTA mothers are frequently heard commenting on the fact that they are asked to bring casseroles and main dishes to school potlucks, while the working mothers are asked to supply items they can pick up on their way home from work—bread, cold drinks, or paper plates.

Sometimes mothers are not asked to do certain jobs because they work. The person at home is not given this consideration. For the same illogical reasons, husbands, children, other relatives, neighbors, churches, and community groups often have very high expectations for the at-home mother. A husband returning home after work, looking around the toy-cluttered living room, and making a comment like, "Hi, Honey. What have you been doing all day?" can be compared to a man entering a gas chamber with a lighted match. There is bound to be an explosion. Mothers know that toys can be picked up a dozen times during the day, but if someone enters through the front door, they *will* be on the floor. That rule is somewhat kin to Murphy's Law: If anything can go wrong, it will.

Neighbors are guilty, also, of high expectations when they make comments like, "Since you are going anyway, would you mind picking up my daughter at school if it rains?" While this may not be an inconvenience once or twice, a steady stream of such requests may become annoying. Often the more accommodating a person is, the more frequently friends will impose. They may even be so bold as to voice their own conclusions, saying, "Well since you are home all day, I know you won't mind." What they are really saying is, "I'm busy; but I know you don't have that much to do."

Falling into this same category will be the mother who will ask if her child may play at your home. You may not mind having other children around, since your house is child-proof anyway. However, your blood pressure may have a right to rise when she tells another neighbor, "Why don't you send Adam to Mary's house? She has so many kids there all the time, one more won't make any difference." What this person doesn't seem to recognize is that you can have eight of your own who know the house rules, and they will not cause one-tenth the trouble one neighborhood child may cause who does not play by the same rule book.

The list of expectations placed on mothers who are at home can go on and on. Jane, a young mother of two small children, told her husband that she wanted to go back to work. When he looked shocked and asked why, she said, "If I work, I will have a reason for not doing all the things that are asked of me. I just don't have the energy to stay at home and be available to everyone who needs something." To enjoy being at home, these mothers need to review the same previously given ten steps that the working mother uses before making a commitment.

Another category of women need to be particularly sensitive to expectations placed on them. They are the working-at-home mothers who are different from the at-home mothers who work. These working-at-home mothers are earning money but doing it from their homes. Women in this category may be employed or self-employed as consultants, writers, direct-mail businesswomen, computer operators, piece-meal workers, artists, or almost any type of worker who is capable of working out of her own home. These women are often seen as very skilled professional women and are in demand to hold voluntary positions on school boards, to chair committees, to head up community drives, to serve on the city council, and to host various civic affairs in their own homes.

Susie was one of these women. She worked at home, and enjoyed it. She was an artist who sold her paintings locally and hoped to expand sales to other states in the near future. As soon as her three children boarded the school bus each morning, she climbed the stairs to her bright, cheerful studio, which had been a dark, dirty attic until fresh paint and a skylight transformed it. She worked without interruption until noon, when she went downstairs to eat her lunch and return any phone calls left on her answering machine. After lunch she returned to her studio and worked until the children came home from school. Her workday ended at 3:30, and the remainder of the day was spent doing housework, preparing dinner, helping with homework, and attending evening meetings. Her husband and children shared in these activities as any other family does—or should do—when it has two working parents.

"Mothers need to use their time wisely. It is so much easier to do this when you are organized. I couldn't get through my day if I didn't organize as I go along." —DEBBIE QUINN

Susie had found a balance between working at home and being an at-home mother. When asked how she did it, she commented, "I learned the hard way through trial and error. At first, I ran down the stairs every time the phone rang. I was afraid to not answer it because I thought one of the children might be ill at school and need me to come. I found that I was a slave to the phone. Since I didn't leave the house every morning and go to work, people assumed I had time to talk. Even when the phone call was only a wrong number, I found I lost a lot of time because I would see other things I needed to do before I returned to the attic.

"I solved that problem by having a telephone with an unlisted number installed near my work area. That number is known only to my husband and children and is used strictly in case of an emergency. It gives me the assurance that I can be reached if needed. The other important lesson I learned was to treat myself like a working woman, and not try to do everything. When I first started working, I felt I was supposed to keep the house spotless because, after all, I was at home all day. I put other expectations on myself as well. It was hard for me to give up control of my duties. Life became enjoyable only after I learned to delegate and not feel the need to control so much. I actually think the children are happier because I'm more relaxed and not as demanding. Keeping the house in perfect order isn't as important to me as it was at one time. We all work to keep it clean, but spotless it is not."

Let's contrast Susie to Ellen, who is working at home as a public relations consultant. Ellen is a very capable, energetic person. She applies her knowledge of public relations to her own business, and her income has doubled in a short period of time. Because she is very visible in the community and is recognized as a person who knows how to get things done, she is asked to serve on many different committees. As her own business has grown, so have her civic commitments. During the day, she works at home, but in the evening when her husband and children are there, she is usually at some meeting. She recently overheard her twelve-year-old daughter telling a friend on the telephone, "My mother is beautiful. Everyone loves her, and I do too, but I wish she was more like your mother. You know the kind I mean—a mother who comes home from work at five o'clock." Up until that time, Ellen had felt she was very fortunate to have her life so well organized. After she overheard her daughter, though, she began to take another look at what she was doing. She realized that her work was not what was interfering with her home life; her civic duties were. As important as her role was in the community, she decided to limit her duties to one night a week. She had gotten caught up in activities that were leaving too little time for her to enjoy her home, husband, and children.

Women like Ellen may overextend themselves for a number of reasons: 1) They have unrealistic expectations of themselves, 2) they do not realize their actions are creating a problem, 3) they do not know how to say no, 4) they rationalize that the situation will only be temporary, and 5) they compare themselves to other women and feel guilty if they are not doing as much as someone else.

Realistically, some situations cannot be easily dealt with by the working mom. There are times when a job puts more demands on her than she can meet. If this is happening and she cannot remedy it, and neither can she quit because of financial reasons, then she must evaluate where in her life she can adjust other time commitments. To plunge ahead without releasing other constraints or tensions is often courting disaster.

Whether the unmanageable expectations are being placed on the working mother by her husband, family, job, church, school, civic organization, or herself is somewhat irrelevant. What really matters is that she recognizes something must be done to correct the situation. After coming to this realization, she must then accept the responsibility and take action to correct the problem. However difficult the situation may be, correcting it will be worth the effort. Expectations of the mom must be realistic if she is to have real joy at work or at home.

3

Choosing the Right Job

Melanie got up at six o'clock every morning, showered, dressed, and cooked breakfast for her husband Tom and her two preschool children. At seven o'clock she woke the children, and the family sat down together for a fast, fifteen-minute breakfast. Then she quickly helped the children get dressed while Tom tidied the kitchen. By 7:30, the family was in the car heading for the nursery school where two-year-old Tom, Jr. and three-year-old Ann would spend their day. After saying goodby to the children, Tom and Melanie drove another three miles to the electronics company where Tom worked and the nearby bank where she worked.

Until six months ago, Tom had worked as an engineer at his company's home office in Texas. Because the California branch was just opening and the career opportunities seemed too good to pass by, he and Melanie had sold their new, three-bedroom, two-bath brick home, and moved. When they arrived in the Los Angeles area and started looking for a house to buy, they quickly realized the real estate market was very different from the one they had just left. A house similar to the one they had just sold would cost nearly twice as much. They could not buy a house until they saved more money, so for the time being they had to rent an apartment.

Melanie had been a first-year schoolteacher when she met Tom five years ago. She had found her work challenging and looked forward to each day she spent with her fourth-grade class. She had continued to work after she and Tom married, but had quit two years ago when Tom, Jr. was born. Working when she had only Ann had seemed fine with Melanie; but the prospects of managing a new baby, plus a one-year-old toddler and a job wasn't something she wanted to tackle. And she didn't have to. Of course, they wouldn't have as much money to spend, but that was all right. They had their new home, and Melanie was very content to wait on decorating it. She told herself that it would probably be better anyway to get new furniture after the children were a little older. So for the past two years, she had stayed home, been a full-time wife and mother, and loved it. Life was good, and Melanie felt joyful and blessed. Then Tom transferred.

Melanie and Tom had always lived on a budget, managed their money well, and avoided the financial worries many of their newly married friends seemed to have. Tom's salary was higher now than it had been at his previous job; but it was only a short time before Melanie realized that with the higher living costs, they would barely make it from one paycheck to the next. If they ever wanted to buy a house, she would have to go back to work. They would need to save enough money to double the amount they already had from the sale of their previous home. A down payment on a house for them would be very expensive in California.

Melanie had presumed that she would go back to teaching when she returned to work; but when she talked to the personnel director in the school district nearby, she learned she would need to take a couple of additional classes to qualify for California teaching credentials. Feeling she could not delay going back to work, Melanie decided to look elsewhere for a job. It was Tom who had suggested that she apply at the bank near his office. Since they had not wanted to drive two cars across country, they had sold Melanie's before they left Texas. By working only a few blocks apart, they would not have to replace her car. Since Tom worked longer hours, Melanie could drop him off at his work, drive to her job, pick up the children when she got off from work, and return later to get Tom.

The plan worked as it was supposed to: Getting by with only one car was manageable, saving for a home was on schedule, and the children were happy in their nursery school. Everything was as near perfect as it could be—with one big exception. Melanie hated her job. The first few weeks were miserable for her, but she thought she would adjust in time. After all, she had worked at only one other job in her life, and that one was in her chosen profession.

But the job did not get better with the passing of time. Melanie just became more depressed. She now felt guilty for not being able to make herself like what she was doing. She told herself that things could be much worse. After all, the people she worked with were very nice, her boss seemed to think she was doing her job well, and she didn't need to take any work home with her. Yes, things could definitely be worse. Even with this kind of pep talk to herself every morning, though, she found she was dreading her days more and more. If it were necessary for her to be away from her own children, then she wanted at least to be with other children in a classroom. While most of her co-workers found banking to be stimulating and interesting, Melanie did not share their enthusiasm. She realized the job that was right for one person was not right for another.

It wasn't long before Melanie's unhappiness began to carry over to her home life. She found herself resenting the enthusiasm Tom had for his job. He had always shared the highlights of his day with her, but he found himself doing it less and less. Sharing with her had been fun before, but now she didn't seem interested.

Melanie could hardly wait until quitting time came each day and she could pick up her children. Even the "terrible twos" had never seemed terrible to her. Being with Ann and Tom, Jr. was sheer joy for her. She still felt the same way; but she found herself being less patient with them than she ever had been before. Things they did that she once would have smiled at were now getting on her nerves.

Fortunately, Melanie and Tom had always had a good talking relationship. They listened to each other and respected one another's thoughts and feelings. Three months after Melanie had gone to work, they remained at the breakfast table on a Saturday morning after the children had completed their meal and left the room. For the next half-hour they discussed Melanie's frustration with her job. Then, for the following hour, they looked to see what options were available to change the situation. It would be at least another year before they would have enough money saved to buy a house. Would it be possible for Melanie to continue for that length of time? And realistically, would it be possible for her to quit even after they had the money saved for a down payment? Wouldn't owning a new home incur new bills?

Tom and Melanie talked until they had arrived at a plan that was acceptable to both of them. Melanie would quit her job and stay at home with the children. Two nights a week, when Tom was home to baby-sit, she would attend night school and take the courses necessary for her teaching credentials. If they needed to use some of the money in savings to pay for tuition and books, they would use it. They would wait to buy the house. In a year, Melanie would be able to get a teaching job, and then a year or two later they would buy a house. In the meantime, they would continue to live in their apartment, as crowded as it was, because by doing so both Tom and Melanie would be spending their days doing what they each enjoyed.

How one's job is going is usually a true indicator of how one's life is going. A job which is done without enthusiasm soon leads to other times of the day being affected in the same way. Tom and Melanie were perceptive in realizing this before their home life was in too much trouble. Not only did they recognize there was a problem, but they did something to correct it.

Many mothers are in jobs they do not enjoy, but they (1) do not want to make sacrifices in their lifestyle to correct the problem, (2) do not know what to do and therefore do nothing, (3) see the problem as only temporary, erroneously thinking things will get better soon, or (4) they have tried to work out something else, but for the time being there is nothing else they can do except stay in their present job.

The latter position may be where many mothers find themselves; but they need to continue working diligently at finding a way out of a miserable situation. Fathers, as well as mothers, need to be aware of the high cost paid by the entire family when the mother is not involved in work which is stimulating and rewarding. Dull jobs often produce dull people, and a mother needs to be alert, happy, and interesting to be around. This same principle applies to mothers working at home, as well as those in the marketplace. If a mother is not fulfilled being at home all day, she needs to look for stimulating things to do, first at home and then in her community. If she does not find them, maybe she needs to see what is available to her on a part-time or full-time basis in the work world.

Some mothers may argue that they must stay at home to be with the children, no matter how they feel about it, themselves. They believe taking care of the children is their duty. Other mothers say they must work outside the home without regard to their preference. Various statistics do tell us that most mothers who work in the marketplace do so because it is financially necessary.

Whether you work outside or inside the home is a decision you will make based on many circumstances. However, a mother needs to be happy in whatever decision she makes. She also needs to have the support of her family and friends and not be judged for her decision.

Cynthia was not only valedictorian of her high-school class, but she also scored very high on her scholastic aptitude tests. After applying to three or four of the top schools in the country, she received acceptances from each one.

Four years later, Cynthia graduated at the head of her class from a very prestigious university, and was accepted into a law school of equal recognition. Her senior year she belonged to the Law Review where she met Richard, a fellow student who would become her husband after graduation.

Cynthia worked for two years after her marriage; but when her first child was born, she decided not to return to work. By this time, Richard was established in a law firm, and his income was sufficient to allow Cynthia to stay at home; he supported her decision. The people who did not were both sets of parents. They were all very pleased about having a new grandchild, but they were not ready to see Cynthia give up her career.

Cynthia's parents had actively supported her during the years she prepared herself to be a lawyer. They were very proud of her dedication and achievements. Answering questions from friends and neighbors about their daughter was a happy experience. Richard's parents also were very proud of their son and of the wife he had chosen. They often marveled at how bright the future was for the young couple. With both of them working, they would be able to have a nice home, luxury cars, fine clothes, and a country club membership much earlier in life than had either set of parents.

When the baby was six weeks old and Cynthia's maternity leave was up, she told her mother she didn't want to leave the baby. She had made an application at a very exclusive daycare center before the baby was born, and she felt excellent childcare was not a question. However, she simply did not want to miss the joy she felt while taking care of her baby. Her mother was shocked. She understood how nice it was to be at home with a new baby because she had stayed at home with Cynthia and her younger brother; but she had not had a career to give up. How could Cynthia give up something she had worked so hard to obtain? After seeing how serious Cynthia was about her decision, her mother offered to baby-sit the child herself at Cynthia's home. Surely this convenience to Cynthia would make her change her mind, the mother thought. But it didn't. Cynthia stayed at home.

Richard and Cynthia had expected their decision to be questioned by some of their professional friends, too, and they were right. One woman expressed real sympathy to Cynthia when she said, "I'm so sorry things have turned out like this for you. Richard must be a real male chauvinist to insist that you stay at home with the baby." When Cynthia told her the decision was hers and that she was very happy being at home, the friend shook her head in disbelief.

"Society puts so much pressure on us mothers. It always seems to tell us we should be doing more." —NANCY TERRELL

Cynthia did not let peer or parent pressure change her mind. She had thought she might go back to work in a couple of years; but by that time her second baby had arrived. When asked now when she plans to go back to work, she laughs and says, "Maybe when I'm about forty." In the meantime, she plans to continue enjoying the only career she wants at the present time, that of being a wife and mother.

Let's face it, though. All women who become mothers do not find the same enjoyment from taking care of babies and small children that some mothers do. One mother expressed her frustration when she said, "I don't know why people judge how good a mother I am by the number of diapers I change. I think I can be just as good a mother, maybe even better than some, by only changing diapers when I get home in the evening and on weekends. As long as my daughter is well cared for when I'm away, I don't feel any less a mother than I would if I stayed home with her all day. I don't need to be with her every minute. In fact, I think I enjoy her more because I'm not with her constantly." Again, we see that choosing the right job is an individual matter, whether that job is away or at home.

Some other factors to consider before accepting a job which will keep you away from home are: (1) Does the job allow you time off for your children's special events? (2) Does it provide nursery care for preschool children?

(3) Does it allow your children the opportunity to become a part of your working world?

Before we start to discuss these three questions, some of you may be saying, "Dream on. Who can ever find a job like that?" You may not have a job that provides any of the three now; but that doesn't mean you may not be able to find one in the future. Knowing that some jobs like this do exist will increase your awareness of things to look for when interviewing for your next job.

Let's look at the first question concerning time off for special events in your child's life. Having a parent at the school play, the Little League game, or a spelling contest can be very important to the child who is participating in that event. Some parents are able to attend these functions, while others are not.

Several factors may make the difference between your attendance being possible or impossible:

1. *The distance from your work to your child's activity.* If you are fortunate to work near the school, the sports field, the church, or wherever your child may be participating in the event, then getting there is easier. However, if your work is in another community or city many miles away, then travel time alone would probably stop you from attempting to go. You might spend more time on the road than you would at the event.

2. *The nature of your work.* If your job allows you to do your work at any time in the day just so long as you get it done, you could probably leave for an hour and make up that time by staying an extra hour at the end of the day. A bookkeeping position might be one example of a job in this category. However, if you are working in an area where other people are depending on your presence, then it would be more difficult to leave. An example of this might be a doctor or a nurse working in a hospital.

3. *How family oriented your company or boss is.* Some companies have very liberal rules about flexible time schedules, particularly if time off pertains to the family. Others do not. If there are no set company rules, your boss

may allow you to leave for a hour or two if he or she understands how important it is to you and your child. If it is important, let your boss know.

4. *The amount of time you have already had off.* If you are on the job every day and take time off only rarely, you usually have a better chance of having your request honored. If your boss has been especially lenient in this area, try not to abuse the privilege. Look at your child's school or sports calender weeks in advance, so you can plan ahead.

5. *How crucial you are to the job and your company.* In other words, if you fill a position where trained workers are in demand and your boss realizes how difficult it would be to replace you, then you may have more bargaining power. Be sensitive to the fact that you may lose in the end if you place too many demands on a boss just because you know you can. Remember, bosses do not like to be put "over a barrel."

The second question pertains to the company providing childcare. If you lived in Sweden, France, Japan, South Korea, or China, finding a company with this benefit would not be difficult. This is especially true of China, where women are expected to work, and childcare is one of the necessities. Companies there provide on-site care which enables mothers to visit their children during the day, usually at lunch or break time. This also is one of the benefits offered by many companies in foreign countries, in the same way health insurance or social security is a benefit in the United States.

> *"I think employers should be more supportive of mothers, especially when the children are small. There are times when the mother must be with a child, and the employers need to understand this."* —JUDY SHRADER

Finding companies with built-in childcare may not be as easy in this country as it is in some others, but it is not impossible. In fact, as the demand grows to keep employees on the job and to reduce absenteeism, more companies will provide this service. This has already happened somewhat in the field of nursing because of nursing shortages in the 1970s. To get nurses to go back to work, many hospitals realized they must provide childcare. Today many recruitment advertisements list this as one of the benefits the hospital provides.

Hospitals have not been the only companies to meet this need. Childcare may be found in factories, engineering companies, universities, and retail businesses, to name only a few. As more women make this a criterion for accepting employment, more companies will find it necessary to provide the service.

The third question that was mentioned earlier asked if the job allowed your children the opportunity to become a part of your working world. When my children leave for college, I try to visit their campuses sometime during the first semester. When we are miles apart, I want to be able to visualize how the dormitory looks, to see where they study, eat, and sleep. I want to walk through the library because I know they will spend a lot of time bent over books at those tables. I want to walk across the campus and feel the excitement and energy that is generated by thousands of young people brought together in one location. Then when I return home, I feel that I'm not so far away from my child because I can close my eyes and see him or her going about the daily routine on that campus.

This same principle can be applied in reverse. A child can feel secure and close to a mother when she is away if that child knows where she spends her day. Some companies allow the mother to bring the child to work with her for a few hours or even a half-day if the child is old enough to occupy his or her time with some activity so the mother may continue her work. If the child is younger, the husband or childcare provider may want to take him or her to visit Mommy at work and remain only a few minutes.

Some children may spend the entire day every day at their mother's workplace. This was true of my children when they were high-school age. We all spent our day on the same campus, where they attended classes and I worked as a counselor. They became a part of my world in a very positive sense, as I became a part of theirs. In the evening, we were able to discuss the school activities because we were all keenly interested in what the other thought of the school assembly that day, or who would win the football game, or who got the leading roles in the school play.

There was never a generation gap because I knew what the other kids on campus were wearing, some of the things they were thinking and feeling, and the pressures they lived with. I felt thankful that my work allowed me to be a part of my children's world, without them being the focal point. In the same way, I believe they felt comfortable being a part of my work world and maybe understanding things from the school's point of view.

Of course, there were certain rules which we all abided by: When I was at school I did not wear my "mother hat"; in fact, some teachers I had worked with for years were surprised to find that the child in their classrooms with my last name belonged to me. I rarely talked about any of my children in the faculty lounge, as they did not discuss me with their peers. We all felt this kept things on a more professional basis. Before I began my work at the school, the family discussed the implications it would have on the children. Jokingly, I told them that I would try to never do anything on campus which would embarrass them, if they would agree to never do anything that would embarrass me. And with the exception of one or two little slips, we all were able to accomplish this goal.

I know that all working mothers cannot work for their children's school system and be a physical part of their world; but mothers can discuss their jobs and let the children know how they spend their day. By sharing our days, we are modeling to the young people, and hoping the results will be that they share with us in the same way. This can go a long way in keeping communication open during the crucial teenage years.

Choosing the right job to enhance family relationships will be something to consider all during the years your children are living at home. Some women have made several career changes at different stages of their children's lives in order to keep close family relationships. How you handle your situation may be different from how someone else handles hers. The important thing is if you are not enjoying your children and not enjoying your work, some changes need to be made.

4

Finding Good Childcare

Mothers who work outside the home keep coming up with the same two answers when asked what makes it possible for them to enjoy their work and enjoy their children. Their answers are, "I have good childcare and don't have to worry about my children," and "I have a supportive husband who helps at home." At the opposite end of the spectrum, mothers who seem not to be able to cope mention inadequate childcare and no support at home.

Since childcare is often the first thing mentioned by these mothers, let's take a look at some important aspects of it, beginning with the types of childcare that are available:

1. *A baby-sitter in your own home.* Some mothers say this type of arrangement is the only way they would leave their children. They cite the fact that the children are left in their own familiar surroundings and they do not have to spend the day away from home. Some mothers of very young children feel especially strong about this arrangement, because they do not have to wake the children early in the morning, dress them, and carry them out into cold or wet weather.

One mother said her second child never had colds or earaches because he was cared for in his own home, whereas the first child had been taken to a daycare center each day, and had constantly had a runny nose or cough. When asked if she thought this was because the second child had been left in a warm home or if it was because he was not exposed to other children who might have carried germs, the mother said she believed it was a combination of both.

Jane, a mother of two, said she liked leaving her children in their own home because she felt she had more control over the children's daily routine, compared with an organized schedule her children would have to fit into at a daycare center. She left instructions as to what she wanted done, or left undone, for the children, and made a point to occasionally drop by her home unannounced and observe what the children were doing. "Children have to follow structured days soon enough when they go to school," Jane said. "I don't want my children to start that any earlier than necessary. I want my children to have the flexibility of enjoying unstructured mornings where something new may happen every day, depending on different factors such as health, weather, mood, and desired activity. In other words, I want them to be able to play with their toys the day after Christmas if they want to."

Other mothers argue against leaving the children at home, saying this does not give the educational benefits that being in a daycare center does. Pauline said her three-year-old was much more advanced developmentally than her five-year-old had been at the same age, because the first child had remained at home and the second one had attended preschool. Some mothers dislike having their children remain at home because the house is always a mess when they get home. But others say just the opposite, that the sitter always cleans up the house. One mother said she usually found it cleaner at the end of the day than it was when she left for work in the morning.

Cost of childcare in the home was another factor which mothers seemed to regard as a positive—or a negative.

Leaving one child at home with a sitter cost too much money for some mothers; but when there were two or three children to consider, it seemed to be more economical.

Finding just the right baby-sitter was also a real concern voiced by the mothers who wanted to have this type of an arrangement. They all agreed that Mary Poppins is hard to find; but most believed finding the right person was not an impossible task. Getting recommendations from friends, and friends of friends, seemed to be the way most of them found someone.

2. *A licensed family home.* "I couldn't ask for a better arrangement," said Betty, a young mother. "This licensed home is only two blocks from my house, which makes it very convenient for me to drop my two off each morning on my way to work. Tommy stays there until eight o'clock when the bus comes by and takes him to kindergarten. Melissa stays at the home all day since she is only four. The woman keeps four other children, and it is like one big happy family. I think my children would rather be there than at their own home."

Some parents prefer this type of arrangement rather than a daycare center because it provides a home-type setting similar to their own. They often talk about the caring and love given in these homes, often by younger women who have children of their own and want to earn a little extra money. Or they may be older women whose children are grown and who miss having little ones around. Sometimes in a case like this, a retired husband will be available to help his wife with the children. One single mother was particularly happy to find a home with a retired husband because she found that he served as a male role model for her son.

When listing negatives of licensed family homes, parents often cite the drawbacks of not having the play facilities or the trained professionals that a daycare center may have. Some parents say they like family homes for babies and toddlers, but for three- to five-year-olds they prefer the advantages of the larger peer group and educational programs which a daycare center provides.

You may want to ask these questions when interviewing a home childcare provider:

- What is the cost of the services?
- How many children does she take care of?
- Does she provide the food or does each child bring a lunch?
- What activities are available for the children inside and outside? Is the yard fenced?
- Are educational toys provided?
- Is the home licensed or registered?
- What are the ages of the children cared for in the home?
- What time may the children be left in the morning, and when must they be picked up in the afternoon?
- Are the doors kept locked at all times?
- Are visits by the parents welcomed?

3. *A daycare center.* This center may be provided by the community, the church, or a company where you are employed. These centers are usually set up like nursery schools, with children being grouped together by age. Usually the people who work here have had some early-childhood-education training, and they take a real interest in seeing the children develop. In a good daycare center, part of each day may be devoted to activities such as singing, counting, drawing, coloring, building with blocks, riding tricycles, or playing games such as "let's pretend."

"I would never leave my child in a daycare center," said a young mother of a two- and three-year-old. "I'd be worried to death, after the terrible things I read in the newspapers about what goes on at some of them."

Child-abuse cases have been reported in the newspapers, and naturally these have caused a great deal of anxiety for parents. Because of these issues, many parents have realized they must do a thorough job of checking out the daycare centers before they leave their children, and that they must continue to monitor them afterward. They should also observe their own children carefully for any questionable marks on the skin, and they must listen closely to what the children may say to them, both verbally and nonverbally. A parent may become aware of an abusive situation simply by observing and listening to the son or daughter.

In evaluating a center, a mother cannot judge the type of care her child will get by the friendliness of the director. A charming administrator will be unable to build her business if observing parents find she is treating them one way but the children another. Alison Clarke-Stewart, an authority on daycare in the United States, says that observation of the actual caregiving situation is the parents' best guarantee of quality.

"Childcare is always a big consideration. I've learned that the most expensive care is not always the best care." —NANCY TERRELL

Here are other suggestions for evaluating a daycare center:

- Talk to other parents who use the daycare center and see if they are happy with the services. Try to talk to several parents whose children are the same age as yours. If parents hesitate at any point when answering your questions, follow up on that same question with other parents.
- Notice if the building provides a pleasant environment, including bright, cheerful rooms with controlled temperature. If children's work is displayed on the walls, observe if all the pictures look alike or if individual creativity has been encouraged.
- Look for safety features in the facilities. Are stairs properly covered with nonskid materials? Does the concrete on the playground have a rough finish so it will not be slippery when wet? Are sharp objects and cleaning solutions kept out of the children's reach?

- Observe how clean the facility is. Ask to see the bathrooms and check them for cleanliness and for ample supplies, such as soap, paper towels, and toilet paper.
- Ask to see where the food is prepared and remain to watch the preparation for a few minutes. Request a sample of the food to taste. See if the lunch is served in an attractive manner.
- See what facilities the center has for nap time. Are allowances made for children who require less nap time than others? Does the caregiver allow children to bring their own blankets or stuffed toys to cuddle while going to sleep?
- Notice if the doors have locks, and if these locks are secured during the day. One mother took her child out of a particular center because locks on the doors were never used, and she feared for the safety of her child.
- Observe what play material is available for the children. Is there a wide variety to accommodate children with different likes and dislikes?
- Notice if the children appear to be happy and content. Are they talking with each other and with the caregiver, or is there a lot of crying and quarreling?
- Ask the director to tell you about a typical day at the center.
- Watch the children as they arrive in the morning to see if they seem happy to be coming there.
- Talk to the caregivers and listen for the words they use to describe the children. Do they show a caring, loving attitude?
- See if you have peace of mind after praying about leaving your children at the center. After you have sought God's guidance, trust your own feelings.

If you have decided to work and do not choose to use a sitter in your home, a licensed family home, or a childcare center, there are still other options for you.

Relatives. Some mothers rely exclusively on grandparents, aunts, sisters, or cousins to care for their children. One mother said that she could go to work with complete peace of mind each morning because her own mother was taking care of her child. She never had to worry about the child being mistreated or abused, and she knew her mother would call her if there were ever a question of not knowing how to handle a situation. Grandparents are usually wonderful resources because they enjoy the time spent with the grandchild, and often they will not take money for their services. Most mothers are sensitive to the grandparents' needs and do not abuse the privilege by leaving a child with them at other times, such as weekends.

Au Pairs. Translated from the French, an au pair is a person who does chores and childcare in a household "as an equal," not as a servant. In return, she gets room, board, spending money, and the experience of being in a foreign country as a real resident, not as a tourist.

"Children must get quality care while the mother is away, not a hit-and-miss thing. I think au pairs are wonderful because they live in your home and become a part of the family."
— JUDY SHRADER

Judy Shrader lives in Pasadena, California, and has been employing au pairs for several years. Anne, a girl from Norway, spent thirteen months with Judy's family and has recently just returned home. Arriving a week after she left was Aysun, a girl from Istanbul, Turkey.

Besides Judy, a critical-care nurse at a local hospital, and Ed, a marriage, family, and child counselor, the family includes Tiffany, age twelve, Teddy, age six, and two foster children, Scotty, age two and a half and six-month-old Christy.

"One of the things I wanted to do was to offer love and a home to children who didn't have either," Judy said.

"But I knew I needed help to do that." She contacted Au Pair Home-stay/USA, a service set up on the East Coast by the Experiment in International Living. "This is absolutely the only way to go," Judy says. "Because of its careful screening on both sides of the ocean, it protects both the au pair and the host family."

In the screening process, the interviewers try to match au pairs with families in the same socioeconomic class. The au pair's English must be understandable, and she must agree to spend forty-five hours a week doing household and childcare duties. In return, the host family provides her with room and board, a hundred dollars a week in spending money, and certain days off.

Baby-sitting co-op. Mothers often join with other mothers in their neighborhoods to form a baby-sitting time to be shared by each mother. This takes several mothers who are willing to participate, and it works better if the mothers work only part time. The secret of this arrangement is that each person is dependable and is committed to making it work. Five mothers may wish to participate, with each mother planning to baby-sit all the children for one day a week. Four days a week her children are cared for by the other four mothers individually and she is free to go to her job. One of the benefits of this is that no money is paid to anyone.

If you have found the childcare arrangement which meets your need, as well as that of your child, test it out first. Have a dress rehearsal, just as if you were going to work, and see what problems come up that week. This should give you a chance to work out any minor obstacles before the plan is actually implemented.

Also before you begin work, sit down and make a backup list of what to do when things go wrong. You may be fortunate and never need to refer to your list; on the other hand, you may need to look at it the first week. Your sitter may get sick, your child may come down with the chicken pox, your car may break down, or you may be asked to work past the time the childcare center closes.

Whatever the situation may be, you need to think about it ahead of time and have a plan for how you will deal with it. If, in a pinch, you are going to need to call on a neighbor, ask about this before you actually need her. In case your mechanic may be busy on the day your car breaks down, have the name of another shop on file. Being prepared eliminates a lot of anxiety when things begin to unravel.

Time and effort should be put into getting just the right care for your child. Remember that each child is different, and you should try to suit the childcare situation to the needs of each individual child. Spend the time and effort to get a workable arrangement. Only when your child is in an environment where he or she is happy will you be able to enjoy your work and enjoy your child, without feeling guilty.

"Children broaden your horizon. They keep you young. They are a joy to the world."
— Ann Bengford

Latchkey Children

Parents sometimes feel their childcare worries are over when the children become school age and are away from the home most of the day. They give the child a key to the house and feel confident everything will be okay for those few hours between when the child and the parent arrrive home, or when a child is home alone all day during the summer. Unfortunately, this is not always true, especially of young school-age children. Police Sergeant Dan Forester says, "No children under eight years old should be left to fend for themselves. If anything happens to such latchkey kids, parents could be prosecuted for felony child endangering and negligence."

He goes on to state, "There really is no age factor in child endangering laws. It depends on the ability of the child."

While some ten-year-olds are more responsible than twelve-year-olds, a parent must make the decision whether to leave the child alone based on each child individually. Many children are quite capable of looking after themselves, if parents take time to teach them about the dangers posed by strangers, as well as potential problems around the house.

Sergeant Forester offered the following suggestions for parents of latchkey children:

- Children should contact parents, neighbors, or relatives as soon as they get home from school.
- Parents should ask neighbors to periodically check on children.
- Children never should enter a house if they see an open door or broken window.
- Kids never should open doors to strangers.
- Kids should be encouraged to tell parents about unusual occurrences involving strangers.
- Children should know how to reach parents at all times.
- Parents should teach kids about the 911 emergency number, or about other emergency numbers if the 911 system is not available.
- Kids should turn on the television set or stereo to give the impression someone else is home.
- Parents should take time to teach kids to safely operate appliances like ovens and heaters.

5

Giving Support to Your Children

In interviewing mothers across the country who have raised happy, well-adjusted children, one central theme seems to always come forth: the importance of giving support to the children. Some of these mothers work outside the home; some do not. But all make the time to be supportive.

One mother talked about keeping baked goods in the freezer and bringing them out just before the children got home from school. An afternoon tea party involving the mother and her children became routine. During that time, she listened to the happenings of each child's day. While having cookies and milk (or a non-sugar snack) is common after school for a lot of children, the difference in this situation was that the mother actively participated with her children. The unspoken message was that the mother cared and thought what her children had to say was important. She wanted to listen. A pattern was set, and no matter what happened in the years to come, the children felt they could talk to their mother about it.

Working mothers will say, "But I'm not at home when the children arrive. What can I do to establish this same bond?" Richard Baltzell told me that his mother had the same routine each day when she came home from work. She went directly into the living room, sat on the couch, took off her shoes, and asked her son to come in and tell her about his day. Richard has grown children of his own now, but he still remembers the thoughtfulness his mother showed to him when he was a young boy.

Home is where the family relaxes, where masks are taken off, and where real communication can take place. One of the main ways that a mother can support her children is by listening to them. According to an article in the National Association of State Boards of Education publication,

> Good communication within the family is the foundation for the mutual trust that encourages responsibility. When parents and children are able to communicate well, they find it's much easier to resolve conflicts and to arrive at mutually agreeable decisions. To communicate effectively, parents need to express accurately to their children their own ideas and feelings as well as to listen to and understand the youngsters' thoughts and emotions. Adolescents, even more than younger children, need someone who will listen. They need a sounding board off which to bounce developing ideas, and they need someone with whom to talk out their problems.

Sally, a mother of two boys ages eleven and thirteen, states, "I know I need to listen to my children, but they aren't exactly at the age to sit and talk. They are very active and seem to always be on the run. Should I just wait until they get a little older, when they are more ready to sit down and carry on a normal conversation?" The answer is no, of course. If you aren't in the habit of talking to your children when they are younger, they won't automatically start talking to you when they are older.

To carry on good conversation does not mean that two people must always sit in chairs and face one another. Some of the best communication may take place in the kitchen when Mom is preparing dinner and daughter or son is helping. Casual conversation is often more relaxed and things are shared that might not be if the discussion is seen as "a big deal."

> *"I try to give each of the boys special attention so neither feels a need to compete for my time. I think this is one reason why they enjoy each other so much."*
> —Vicki Rockett

Sally, the mother of two sons who are "always on the run," might take her cue of when to communicate from looking at where she spends time with them, which is in the car driving them from one activity to another. True, the conversation may be terminated earlier than she wished because they arrive at their destination, but some sharing is better than none. Also, there are many advantages to being in a car: There are no interruptions by the doorbell or telephone (unless you have a car phone); no one can decide to walk out on the conversation; and the car is often the initial place a child may be after an upsetting event, such as losing a game.

Another form of support is sharing. Some families have decided to set aside one night a week or one Saturday or Sunday afternoon to be used as sharing time. This does not mean, necessarily, that sharing refers to talking. It may mean participating in an activity together. One mother said she had no interest in putting puzzles together until she started doing it with her daughter as a shared activity. She found that soon she was looking forward to every Thursday evening, not particularly because she had grown to like the puzzles, but because she really enjoyed spending the time with her daughter.

The story is often told of the father who took a day off from work one summer in order to take his son fishing. The father didn't feel the day went very well, because neither of them caught any fish. He had actually found it to be a rather boring day and thought he had probably wasted his time in taking the day off. It wasn't until many years later when the father was sitting in the audience of a high-school graduation ceremony and listening to his son give the valedictory speech that he realized how wrong he had been. His son described each detail of the day, from early morning to late in the evening. Tears came to the father's eyes as he heard his son say how much he had enjoyed that day and how important the support of his father was to him.

Time spent with sons and daughters is an investment in the future; but the positive impact it makes is not always known. However, if time is not spent, the negative impact will definitely be seen. This fact was very apparent to me as I worked with various distraught parents of high-school students who had gotten into trouble. These fathers and mothers were not at school because they found it convenient to take time off from work, but because they had been summoned. As the parents and the student sat in the office together, I often thought what a shame it was they were having to spend time together in this way. How much better it would have been if they could have spent the same amount of time together earlier in a happy situation. I truly believe that parents who do not spend time with their children in a positive way probably will spend time with them later in a negative situation.

I believe some students get into trouble at school just to get their parents' attention. How much better it would be if those same students felt they had their parents' support and did not need to act out in a negative way to get it.

Parents can show support to students at school in many different ways. Some ways take a great deal of time; others take very little. Just showing an interest in the school life of the youngster is an example of simple but meaningful support. Caring enough to ask how he or she feels about the semester, how the classes are going, or what activities are scheduled will show your interest. Unfortunately, the only time some parents ask questions is when the report card comes home, and then the questions are often inflammatory, asking "Why didn't you get better grades?"

Some people think they must participate in an active organization to show support for the school and their child; but there are many other ways. The immigrant parent of a ninth-grade girl expressed this concern when she said, "I speak only a little English, and I don't feel comfortable in groups like the PTA. Is there anything else I can do?" In fact, she was already showing support—by attending every basketball game her daughter's team played. The daughter sat on the bench most of the games, but that didn't matter to the mother. She was there to see her daughter play the few minutes she was on the court. Her support was unwavering.

"I always considered it extremely important to make personal contact with my children's teachers. Establishing a close relationship with a teacher will be one of the most critical things you do for your child." —Bonnie Bear

---

The final year in high school seems to be a time when some parents feel their child no longer needs them. While seventeen- or eighteen-year-olds do appear very grown up, there are many instances when they still need their parents' support. The senior year is a time of decisions: whether or not to go to college, which colleges to apply to, or where to find a job after graduation. High-school counselors try to be available to help students with these dilemmas; but frequently the time a student spends in the counselor's office is very limited due to the sheer number of students assigned to that counselor. The parent needs to be aware how crucial this senior year is. If deadlines are not met, the student may not get into a certain college simply because the application did not arrive on time. If financial aid is needed, the parent will have to help the student fill out the forms, since some of the questions pertain to the parents' finances.

While some parents may look on such duties during their child's senior year as an intrusion into their time, other parents see it as a real blessing. One mother said, "I got to spend more time with Helen this year than I did in the two previous years put together. Before, it seemed her friends were the ones she turned to for advice; but this year she needed my help." Another parent said, "I spent so much time with my son this year in visiting prospective colleges, talking to admission directors, and meeting financial-aid deadlines, I just wonder what happens to the student whose parent doesn't get involved."

Another way to show support for your son or daughter at school is to encourage him or her to participate in school activities, and then continue to show your support by attending these events. A recent survey of what kids remembered most about high school revealed that it wasn't the courses or the grades, but the activities. Many students never know the joy of participating in a play on opening night or of being part of a winning team, because no one encouraged them in the previous months to try out for a spot. Younger children need the same show of support for their activities.

A working mom may need to be a little more creative in ways she shows support if her time schedule is inflexible. However, there are ways to become involved in a son or daughter's activities if one looks for them. That feeling of support makes the effort very worthwhile. For instance, if it is impossible to attend a daughter's softball games because the mom is at work when they take place and she can't get off, that mom might have the team over for hamburgers the night before a big game, or invite them over for a weekend cookout.

The types of support we have been talking about up to this point have been more active than passive. Listen-ing, sharing, and being available demands a certain degree of activity by the parent. Now let's look at another form of support which often is more difficult to do, even if it does demand less of the parent's time. I am talking about being supportive in allowing the young person to make a certain number of decisions for himself or herself, even if we know those decisions are not the wisest ones.

Jenny's mother was a lovely woman with an abundance of intelligence and charm. She used her many talents in a very positive way and could be counted on if help was needed at any of the school functions. Most people in the community seemed to know and like her because she was friendly to everyone. To those who were looking in from the outside, Mrs. Rice was as close to being a perfect mother as anyone would find. But Jenny saw another side to her mother, that of a very controlling woman. Because she was successful at almost everything she attempted, Mrs. Rice didn't have patience with people who made incorrect decisions. Therefore, she reasoned that it was easier to "help" Jenny with her decisions than to allow her to make mistakes. As a result, when Jenny left for college, she was insecure and frightened at the thought of being on her own. Later, making even minor decisions in college created a lot of stress for her.

In contrast, Jason's mother thought children should be involved in making decisions, even from a very young age. When Jason was four she allowed him to select his own shoes; she just made certain the size was correct. By the time he reached high school, making decisions came second nature to him. Most of his decisions were good ones, but he did make a few he wished he hadn't. For example, he quit his part-time job his senior year and later realized he needed more spending money. But when he made a bad decision, he was still at home, and felt safe and secure in trying again and learning from his mistakes. He felt the support of his mother. By the time he left for college, his decision-making skills were developed, and tackling college was not very frightening for him.

The comparison between these two teenagers is extremely revealing. Both came from homes where they were cared for and loved. If asked whether she supported her child, each mother would have answered "yes" without reservation. The difference was Jason's mother knew that support sometimes meant backing away and allowing the young person to take the risk of making his or her own decisions. This may be a different form of support, but it is important. It ranks right up there with listening, sharing, and being involved.

6

Having a Supportive Husband

"Before our first daughter was born, I worked for the United Press in Chicago; but after she arrived I decided to stay home. However, it wasn't long before I felt like I needed something else to do. I really wasn't, and am still not, a person who likes to play bridge or engage in similar types of social activities. While I was still contemplating what I should do, a man from a local newspaper contacted me to see if I'd become their women's page editor, telling me I could work from home most of the time.

"I took the job and started working from home; but it soon became apparent that I needed some household help. I just wasn't the type who could do it all and still retain my sanity. It wasn't until later that I discovered the reason we had money to hire help was because my husband gave up two of his hobbies, flying and playing golf. These were expensive hobbies, and they also took a lot of his time, especially the golf. He felt a real partnership in taking care of our child, so he gave up both of these time-consuming activities. I really didn't know why he had given up his hobbies until a couple of years later. It was never really talked about; but then I found out that he had sacrificed them so

I could have household help, and so he could spend more time with our daughter. That is the true measure of this man."

These words were not spoken by a 1990s young mother describing her modern-day husband who belongs to the current generation of involved fathers. Surprisingly, this woman, Alicia Klauss, was remembering something that happened forty years ago.

In talking to other women with grown children, I found many of them who felt their husbands had been actively involved in child rearing. As one woman explained, "Our husbands did what was necessary to do, but they just didn't talk about it. It wasn't that they hid it, but no one was writing books or articles in magazines in those days to tell them that it was all right to discuss it. It wasn't fashionable then for the men to do 'woman's work.'"

"I don't think there is any such thing as a woman's role. My husband steps in and does everything I do." —JUDY SHRADER

Things have definitely changed in the last two decades. Now it is not only fashionable for men to be involved in parenting and to help with household chores, but it is expected in most homes.

"Wayne and I share equally in the raising of our two young sons, and in the upkeep of the house," states Lynn Walter, an engineer. She and her husband, also an engineer, rotate going to work an hour earlier or an hour later. The one who goes in later dresses, feeds, and takes the two boys to their destination, one to a sitter and the other to preschool. The one who goes to work earlier and gets off first picks up the children and prepares dinner. "For a long time, I was the one who went in later and had the care of the children every morning. Then I realized we should takes turns. Now I am going in early, and I find it much easier. It's much better when we rotate the duties."

Janice Gutierrez, an advertising account representative and sister of Lynn Walter, has similar feelings about child rearing. "I worked until Melissa was born, but Dan and I had made an earlier decision that I wouldn't return to work. We both wanted me home with the baby. I see that now as what I do. I spend my working day as a mother. I'm not staying at home to be a housekeeper—Dan and I share in the household duties just like we did when we were both working at jobs away from home. Dan is also a very involved father. We both want it that way."

> *"I made a decision to stop working, not to be a maid, but to be a mom. Motherhood should not be equated with being a housekeeper."*
> — JANICE GUTIERREZ

Dawn Brainard, a data operations analyst, describes her husband admiringly, "Mark is one of six children, and his mother taught each child to do his or her share of the housework. When Mark and I married, he already knew how to do everything around the house, so it was just natural for us to share the duties. When our son was born, sharing in parenting duties came without question."

Not all modern mothers have such supportive husbands as Lynn, Janice, and Dawn. For some, it is a constant struggle to get their husbands to share the load, even when the mother works outside the home.

Martha, a secretary and mother of two, says, "Jim thinks that he is doing me a favor every time he helps with the housework. He doesn't look at it as being both our responsibilities. He sees it as my work, and he thinks he's being real considerate by giving me a hand sometimes."

Lisa, a former schoolteacher and mother of four, says, "Steve was wonderful to help me when I was working at school; but once I quit and stayed home full time, he stopped helping. At night when he is relaxing in front of the television, I am still working. He doesn't seem to understand that I can't get everything done in an eight-hour day."

> *"When you work, you are so stressed out, so tired, and to me it seems a woman's work never stops. A man can work his eight hours, go home, and clock out with TV or fishing; but a woman can never do that. A working woman changes hats so many different times, and her work is never ending."*
> —MARCIE PERRY

Other mothers have been able to make changes in their households and their once-reluctant husbands are now becoming more willing to help and more proficient at being supportive. As one young mother put it, supportive husbands are made, not born. Some of the ways these mothers have guided their husbands into a more supportive role are described below:

1. *Give your husband praise when he helps.* Virginia, a mother of a one-year-old says, "When my husband first started helping with the baby, he was awkward and clumsy because he'd never cared for a baby before. But as he made the slightest improvement at changing diapers or feeding our daughter, I would always make a point of telling him how well he was doing. The praise was genuine because he really was improving, and I was proud of him. As he became more successful at caring for her, he started to enjoy it more, and, thereafter, wanted to do more things for her. It's the same thing that most of us feel. If we think we are doing a good job, we enjoy our work. I think it is very important to let husbands know they are doing a job well, no matter if it is caring for a child or vacuuming the floor."

2. *Let your husband know you need help.* "I just let my husband know that I cannot do it alone," says Tina, a mother of a newborn. "Before we got married, we attended an engaged couples seminar sponsored by our church, and we

talked about what our expectations were after marriage. I know some of my friends were hesitant about letting their fiancés know how much they expected of them in helping around the house and parenting; but I was completely honest with Mike. I figured if he didn't like what he heard, it was better for me to know it then than later." Jokingly she continued, "He probably really didn't comprehend all he was agreeing to at the time; but he certainly knows now. To me, it is just so much easier to tell Mike that I need his help than it is to do the work myself and let resentment build up."

3. *Give your husband a plan to work by.* "I think men work better when they have a plan to go by," says Helen. "I know Bill is a very structured person, and in his accounting job he works in a very orderly and concise way. I try not to throw him off base by having him work differently at home. We both sit down on weekends and make our schedules for the following week. Not only do we list what we each are supposed to do, we also discuss how we will go about doing it. When we first got married, these discussions were really more important than they are now because our duties are more familiar to us. We even talked about what solution was best to use to clean the kitchen floor and if it should or should not be rinsed.

"This may sound unnecessary, but it has alleviated a lot of problems before they developed. I'm thinking of a friend who asked her husband to mop the kitchen floor, and she became furious when she walked on the floor later and found it sticky to her shoes. The poor guy didn't know what he had done to make her so mad—he didn't know he was supposed to rinse after mopping. However, she was never able to get him to mop again. The experience had left him with too many unpleasant memories. To me, it is just easier to avoid those pitfalls."

4. *Let your husband know he is still very special in your life.* "I firmly believe that husbands are more willing to share in all phases of housework and child rearing if they feel they are loved and cherished," said Wanda.

"You're so right. When we are so very busy with work, home, and children, I think we need to be careful not to forget about the special things we did for our husbands before we had children," said Monica, the mother of two.

Wanda continued, "I remember how I use to have surprises for Ned. I was always doing something to make him know I really cared about him, and he loved it. A few months ago, I was thinking how long it had been since I'd surprised him with anything. You know how easy it is to get busy and just try to keep your head above the water doing the daily, routine chores. Well, I remembered Valentine's Day was coming up soon, so I made arrangements to leave the kids at Grandma's house on the weekend before the holiday. I made reservations at a hotel on the beach, and paid for it with some money my parents had given me for a Christmas present. I will never forget Ned's expression when I picked him up from work on that Friday afternoon. Instead of having two kids in the car with me, I had our suitcases all packed and ready to go. It wasn't even necessary for us to go back home. We just took off to the beach.

"Ned said he hadn't felt so young and free in a long time. He said it made him feel like he was in high school again and was going to the beach without a worry in the world. We walked on the beach, roasted hot dogs in a fire we built at a picnic area, watched the late show on television, and slept late the next morning. The one thing we didn't do was talk about the kids. For that one weekend there was just the two of us again. Of course, by the end of our mini-vacation, we were both eager to get back and see the children again, but the memories of that weekend have stayed with us."

"I haven't done anything quite that special, but I do try to do little things," Monica said. "When Patrick goes away on a business trip, I pack little love notes all throughout his suitcase. If I know he's presenting a paper or an idea at a big meeting and he's tense about it, I may write a note that says, 'You're the greatest. I know it, and after the meeting they're going to know it too.' I place the note in the pocket of his best white shirt because I know he will find it when he's getting dressed. Several times he's told me that my notes gave him that extra word of encouragement that he needed."

"This may sound like bribery, but I don't mean it that way," said Michelle, a new mother. "Some nights when we get the baby down, I ask Charles to help me with the remaining chores. I tell him if we get them done quickly, I'll give him a head and shoulder massage. He just can't resist that offer. It gives us time to talk, which I enjoy, and at the same time, he is feeling like I am doing something especially for him."

5. *Arrange for your husband to spend some time with husbands who do share in household duties and parenting.* "Isn't it amazing? If a wife tells a husband something, he doesn't seem to hear it; but if another man says the same thing, it becomes gospel," Mary told her friends laughingly. "Don't get me wrong; I'm not kicking it. I just had to find a way to use it."

"And did you?" her friend Janet asked.

"Yes, I did. And I might add, my life has been happier ever since."

"Let's hear about it," Janet encouraged.

"Well, Stephanie, my college roommate, was always telling me how much Scott helped her. He really sounded too good to be true. I didn't think any husband was that supportive because I hadn't been raised in a home where men helped out. I guess you might say my expectations were rather low because I just didn't know any better. But the more I was around Stephanie and Scott, the more I knew there was a better way of doing things.

"But just how was I going to get my husband to change? I decided to talk to Stephanie about it, and as usual, she had some ideas. She suggested that Fred and I come over for a barbecue one evening and bring our kids. Fortunately, the men hit it off right away when they started talking about football teams, and that was the beginning of many evenings we all spent together. I noticed Fred watching Scott as he helped prepare meals, clear the table, and get the kids to bed. Remember, Scott had already established himself in Fred's eyes as a macho male because he knew all the sports statistics; so seeing him help around the house didn't diminish this image. In other words, Fred still accepted him as a role model. It didn't happen overnight, but gradually Fred began to help without my asking him. He may not help now as much as Scott does; but let me tell you, it's a lot better than it used to be. And we're still spending evenings together with Scott and Stephanie, so I have hopes that it will get even better."

Now that we have heard from women about their feelings of having supportive husbands, let's hear from a couple of men:

Gregory is a marriage, family, and child counselor and the father of two children, ages six and seven. "I don't even like the term 'supportive husband,'" states Greg, "because I don't think that is what a man should be."

Stopping to notice the reaction his statement was bringing, he continued, "To me, if a man is supportive that means he is aiding, helping, or bolstering up his wife. In other words, he is helping her perform her duties. I look at my role as a husband and father as being one of sharing equally with my wife in all areas of our home life. Instead of helping her with the children, I take my rightful place beside her, and we both care for them. If a man looks at it in this light, he will not expect a woman to remind him about his chores any more than he would expect his co-workers at his job to remind him to perform his tasks there.

"This approach not only takes a burden off the wife, it also allows the husband to be actively involved as an equal. The result is he has a greater respect for his wife because he now sees her as an equal, and he has greater enjoyment of his children because he is busily involved with them as part of his role, not as an appendage of the wife."

Bryan, the father of a two-year-old, explains his feelings in this manner: "I have been involved in Sarah's life ever since we found out she was expected. I attended all the childbirth classes with Florence, stayed with her in the delivery room, witnessed Sarah's birth, and have had an active role in parenting her ever since. I wouldn't have it any other way. I think of my own father sometimes and think how much he missed by being at work so much of the time when my brother and I were young. Of course, he was a very successful businessman; but he sacrificed a lot of time at home. For me, personally, I'd rather not achieve so much in my profession and be able to enjoy my family more. I plan to be as much involved with Sarah as Florence is. That also means I will be involved in every aspect of our home life, including doing my fair share of the chores. Being a family man is too important to me to have anyone, or anything, take it away from me."

Many people see men's involvement in parenting as being a new thing. Others see it as a continuation of what their fathers did in the past, but just didn't talk about. For some men, life hasn't changed at all. Their fathers did not help take care of them, and they aren't helping to parent their own children. Others, like Bryan, see what their fathers missed and are making sure they don't make the same mistake, or, at least, not make the mistake they *think* their fathers made.

Having a supportive husband to help with the housework also is seen as something new for some people, but not for others. As more and more women enter the work force, many are asking for help from their husbands so they both may have more time to enjoy each other and their children.

7

Sharing Holidays

"Christmas was always my favorite time of the year when I was a kid, and I want it to be like that for my own children," said a young mother of three pre-teenage youngsters. "But I'm afraid it may not be. My memories include wonderful aromas coming from the kitchen, every room in the house beautifully decorated, friends dropping by, gifts under the tree weeks in advance. Now, contrast that to what my kids experience during the holidays: They see me coming home from work, tossing TV dinners in the microwave, and dashing off to do last-minute shopping before the stores close. Instead of great aromas from the kitchen, they see pies and cakes being brought in from the bakery and even the already-prepared stuffing for the turkey coming out of a box.

"As for the decorations, we are lucky if one room gets done, much less the entire house. Putting up the tree is time consuming enough. And the packages, well they get wrapped on Christmas Eve. The mood around the house is usually anything but happy, because we are all so rushed and tempers are short. When I read the Christmas cards that say, 'have a joyful Christmas,' I just want to stop and ask,

'Now how do you expect us to do that on top of all the other things we have to do?'"

If too much of this story seems familiar, maybe you will want to look for other ways of getting through the holidays. If we have only one time during the year to really enjoy our children, then Christmas should probably be that time.

"That's easier said than done," said Pat, a mother of a six-year-old boy and a five-year-old girl. "I used to enjoy Christmas, too, until I started to work; now I just look at it as a chore, just one other thing in my life that I don't have time for."

"I can identify with Pat's comment," said Judy, another working mother. "There are just so many hours in the day. And if every minute is already taken, how am I expected to enjoy squeezing in additional things like cooking, shopping, writing cards, and receiving guests? I'd be happy seeing Christmas come only every other year."

When working mothers feel this pressured, some of the tension is bound to spill over onto the children. While these youngsters surely have good memories of Christmas, they may not be the same glorious memories their mothers had. Are there ways to make Christmas better and more memorable? I think so. Let's look at some ways:

1. *Do your Christmas shopping all year long.* Start with the fabulous after-Christmas sales. You may want to buy one or two gifts a month, or buy at random as you come across the merchandise. January is a great time to purchase gifts of sheets, towels, or small household goods, because these items are usually on sale then and they will store easily. Gifts of clothing for children may need to be purchased closer to December to assure getting the correct size.

The first year's shopping may take some planning on your part. The Christmas budget will need to be spread out so you will have money in January to purchase gifts for the coming year. The next year will be easier because you will have more presents purchased ahead of time, and the money needed for December will not be so great. The advantages of buying presents all year long are many: (a) You can take advantage of sales, (b) you have more time to look and probably will be able to put more thought into your selections, (c) you eliminate the pressure of having to buy at a particular time, (d) if you travel during the year, you may find very special gifts not available to you in your own city, (e) you avoid the crowds of December, (f) the salespeople have more time to help you, (g) the merchandise selections may be better, (h) you reduce the chance of having to shop in bad weather, and (i) shopping will be one less thing you will have to do during December.

    2. *Address your Christmas cards early.* Many people buy their cards in January when they are half-price. This not only saves money, it places the cards in the home, making them available for addressing any time during the next eleven months. After the card is addressed and signed, leave the envelope unsealed. Before mailing, you may want to include a newsletter with the card. With the accessibility of computers, many moms have gotten very creative in designing their own personalized letters, which will include the many events of the previous year.

    Thirty years ago, I started writing one letter and making copies to include in all my Christmas cards. There was no way I had time to write an individual letter to send with each card, and friends and relatives across the country wanted to hear about the children and our lives in California. When I read in a newspaper column that sending reproduced letters in cards was considered very tacky, I wondered if my friends had rather know the events of the year or have me observe proper etiquette and send only a signed card. I knew which I'd rather receive, myself, so I kept sending the letters and often included a picture of the children. Recently, I found several of those old letters in a box my daughter and I were looking through. She had never seen the earlier letters, and was fascinated by reading about some of the events that had occurred in our lives during those early years. "I wish you'd saved copies of every letter and given them to us kids on our eighteenth birthdays," she said. "Our own family history was recorded in those letters."

Now why didn't I think of that! I would enjoy going back and reading those letters, too, and recalling some of the events that I haven't thought about in years. Keeping her own Christmas letters will be something I'm sure my daughter will do for her children. It also may be something you want to do for yours.

And by the way, I don't think many people consider them tacky. Judging from the number I receive each year, the idea seems to be quite popular. I thought at one time I might start writing individual letters again after the children were grown and I had more time. I haven't. Maybe I will if I ever do have more time. But then I ask myself, why? That time could probably be better used helping a friend who has less free time than I do.

Christmas cards which include a picture can also be saved to record the family's history. I recently visited a friend in her beautifully decorated home, and was delighted to see one stair wall covered with custom-framed Christmas-card photos of the family. For more than twenty-five years, pictures had been taken, recording the growth of the children, the changes in fashion and hairstyles, and the maturing of the parents. This not only created a record for posterity, it also provided enjoyment for anyone who had the good fortune to walk up or down those stairs. As I stood and looked for several minutes, I was particularly attracted to one of the earliest cards, which showed their first child sleeping in his crib, looking like a perfect angel. Inscribed in bold print on the card was one word, "Peace."

While I admired each picture, the mother told the story of how she had carefully saved the cards in a box until she could have them all custom framed at the same time. Just three years previously, the family had designed and built their new home, and at last she was ready to display her cards. Much to her alarm, she found that her husband had unknowingly thrown the box away in preparation for the move. As friends and neighbors across the country heard of her disappointment, they began to search for any of these cards which they might have saved throughout the years.

Happily, with various people returning different cards, the complete collection was soon retrieved, thus making this display even more special, because so many caring people had made it possible.

If you decide to send family-photograph Christmas cards, have the pictures made no later than the first of November. If the children are older and not changing monthly, you may want to have it done even earlier. Waiting until the last minute will just add one more thing to make your holidays hectic.

3. *Bake and freeze.* One year at Thanksgiving I baked too many pumpkin pies, so I wrapped the uncut ones and placed them in the freezer. I had forgotten about them until the day before Christmas, when I was looking for something else in the freezer and happened to see them. How nice it was to have one less thing to bake for Christmas dinner! Every year since then, I've baked double the amount of pies at Thanksgiving and saved half for Christmas. The same thing may be done with other dishes you prepare earlier. I find it much easier to double or even quadruple a recipe than to bake it on two separate occasions. Any food preparation that can be done early and frozen will give you that much more time to enjoy the day with your children and still serve a holiday feast.

> *"I try to be accommodating with my children's families having their own celebrations at Christmas and Thanksgiving. . . . I've found that it really doesn't matter if we celebrate at my house on the exact day of the holiday. The main thing is that we all get together sometime during that week."* — CAROLINE BRAINARD

4. *Turn your Christmas decorating into a family affair.* Somewhere along the way, moms have been told that having a beautifully decorated house was their responsibility.

Let's face it: Decorating may be fun, but it's a lot of work. Why should moms have all the fun (and do all the work) by themselves? Why not give each child, of a reasonable age, certain rooms to decorate? Let each start with his or her own room. The decorations may be simple ones, like pine cones sprayed with glitter, but they will be very special if they are placed by little hands.

Make getting the tree a family tradition. Some families go into the woods to cut their own tree, while others go to tree farms to do the same thing. Probably the majority of us buy them from a lot; but just the selection of the tree can be a family affair. Our tradition is to go to the lots by the railroad tracks in downtown Los Angeles and select one from the hundreds which have arrived in the boxcars. Because the selection is so great, and the children so many, we usually spend close to half a day finding one that everyone agrees on.

Some families have each child place certain ornaments on the tree every year, as a tradition for that child. When the children leave home they take those special ornaments and place them on their own trees.

Some families have tree-decorating parties and include extended family members and neighbors. Still others want only the immediate family present. Whichever way you do it, just make sure Dad and the children are included in the fun. If Mother does it alone, the fun turns into work.

5. *Entertain friends all in one evening.* While small, intimate dinner parties may be wonderful, having several of these affairs during the holidays may involve too much work for Mom. Inviting friends to an open house is probably much easier, especially when there is a cold buffet rather than a formal sit-down dinner. By greeting your guests all in one evening, there is only one preparation and one clean-up time.

The five suggestions given above are meant to save your energy so you will have more time to enjoy your children during the holidays. There are probably many more time-saving ideas which would apply to your own situation.

Before the end of October, sit down and write out five of your own ideas on how you plan to save time and make your next Christmas a little less hectic and a whole lot happier.

While Christmas is an important time for families, other events like birthdays get top billing also. Having someone to share our special occasions with is a part of what a family is all about. Research has confirmed that people who live in families have longer and healthier lives than those who live alone. The family provides its members with a sense of security, the knowledge that they are loved, and the awareness that someone is there to care and help if needed—and to remember their birthdays!

Young children remember birthday parties for years. In fact, no matter how busy a mother may be, she somehow finds the time to send out invitations, purchase party favors and decorations, bake a cake, and then corral a room full of excited, energetic children, either at home or at a fast-food restaurant or amusement center.

Many families also arrange birthday parties for their elder members, too. For example, everyone may gather to celebrate Granddad's seventy-first birthday. It is those years between youngsters and senior citizens, however, that people seem to forget to celebrate. One of the most joyous times for a family is when they gather to celebrate a happy occasion. When the father helps the children to remember the mother's birthday and the mother calls attention to the father's birthday, a pattern is being set for future years of family enjoyment.

One mother uses a special red plate for birthday celebrations. The person who has the birthday gets to eat from the plate that says, "Happy Birthday. You are special." Feeling special one day a year is something everyone can benefit from; but unfortunately, not everyone receives this special attention.

Another mother has a musical plate which rotates on a platform as it plays "Happy Birthday." She tells the story of using this plate for her son's birthday cake each year as he was growing up. After he was married and lived many states away, she decided to visit him one year on his birthday. When he heard that she was coming for the celebration, his only request was, "Mom, don't forget to bring the birthday plate." One never gets too old to relive happy moments.

Birthdays are made special by the love that is revealed through thoughtful acts, not by the expensive presents received. A young wife recalled the year her mother had baked a cake with a doll in the center. The doll's head and upper body were visible, but the lower body and legs were covered by a beautifully decorated bouffant-skirt cake. She remembered helping her mother place each little round candy "red hot" on the border of that shirt—an act of painstaking detail to make this cake special. When I asked the young woman what gifts she had received on that sixth birthday, she thought for a moment and then shook her head. "I can't recall any of the gifts, not even at my party; I just remember that beautiful cake and working beside my mom to decorate it."

"The important thing is to really enjoy your children, to delight in them. To me, how you feel about them makes the difference in how the children feel about themselves."
— JOYCE PENNER

Giving a child a morning or an afternoon of your time may be the gift he or she will remember most. That may mean letting some other things slide for that week, or it may mean just rearranging the time schedule. Jane, a working mother of two, told me she usually did her grocery shopping and errands on Saturday morning until the year her four-year-old's birthday fell on a Saturday. Because she wanted to spend the day with him, she did her grocery shopping on Friday night after the kids had gone to bed and her husband was watching television. She was amazed how empty she found the usually crowded store and how much more relaxed she felt while doing her shopping. "I even enjoyed reading the labels," she commented half-jokingly. From that point on, she shopped either Friday night or Saturday night, depending on which night she and her husband went out. After work during the week, she ran the other errands which were normally saved for Saturday morning. "Because of making time for that one birthday, I actually found that I could have every Saturday morning to enjoy my children," she said.

Christmas and birthdays are times for major celebrations in a family's life; but minor events should not be overlooked, either. A friend told me that she kept poster paper at her house all the time, and when any accomplishment by a family member needed to be noted, she'd make a sign and display it where the person would see it when arriving home. One poster might say, "Nice home run. Next to Hank Aaron, you're the greatest." Another one would have "Congratulations on getting the part. This school play will win an academy award." Or, a sign for Dad might read, "Congratulations on your promotion. Let's go out to dinner and celebrate."

The important thing for both the working mother and the at-home mother to remember is to have supplies available, so that whatever needs to be done can be done quickly. If the poster paper and the pens are easily accessible, writing a sign takes only a few minutes, but the impact can be long-lasting.

Along with paper and pens, a mother may want to stock a closet with balloons, cards, and even gifts which are bought in advance. Emily, a mother of three, said that she had a special hiding place for small, impromptu gifts which she would purchase months in advance and store until the time came for a celebration. Then, rather than having to take time to run out and quickly make a purchase, Emily would go to her supply drawer and choose an appropriate gift for the occasion. Many everyday happy occasions may be celebrated when the mother is prepared and does not need to take a lot of time for minor celebrations.

Next to major and minor celebrations comes another type of holiday: the family vacation. In talking to mothers about ways they enjoy their children, the one thing they all seem to mention is time they spend together on family trips. Camping trips seem to come up the most, since this type of vacation is less expensive than staying in hotels and eating in restaurants. All of those who spend time in the mountains, on the beaches, or just in a favorite spot near home seem to feel that real quality time together takes place on a camping trip. Just remember that this is a vacation for Mom, too; she should not have to do all the work. Cooking, cleaning, setup, and breaking camp should be shared by all members.

Car trips to places like Disneyland, Yosemite, the Grand Canyon, and Washington, D.C. are also mentioned as favorite activities to do as a family. Jeanne and Bob take their four children on a car trip each year, and while Bob drives, Jeanne reads the children a story book about the place they will be seeing. This activity not only makes the time pass quickly in the car, but it also gives the children an appreciation for the sights ahead.

All families have favorite vacations they like to recall, and our family is no exception. The one they seem to talk about the most is the bicentennial trip from California to the East Coast. The children were at a very good age for a trip of this nature with the oldest one being sixteen and the youngest one six. For weeks we had maps spread out, with destinations marked.

The plans were going beautifully until three days before we were to leave. What a blow it was to all of us when my husband came home and told us a major crisis had arisen at his work and he would not be able to leave the project during the next two weeks. Disappointment reigned supreme all through the house.

As typical with most engineers, though, my husband soon came up with a solution to the problem: I would take the children, alone, and make the trip as scheduled. At first, I wondered if I could actually go alone across country with eight children in a station wagon; but the spirit of adventure in me soon squashed any fears. I would do it!

Since we were no longer confined to a two-week trip, we decided to see more places than we had originally planned. I was a school nurse at the time, and like the children, I had the entire summer free. The only restraint was money, not time. So we carefully planned how we could spread out our vacation from two to five weeks and keep it within the proposed budget. I must say we came up with some creative ideas. Some of these may work for you:

1. *We stayed with relatives whenever possible.* Since the children all grew up in California, they had seen their father's relatives in South Carolina very infrequently. What a joy it was for these city children to ride tractors on a farm there.

Before the five weeks were up, we had spent time with my relatives in Texas and Arkansas, and Roy's relatives in South Carolina and Washington, D.C. When we were at each place, we tried to see all the sights in the area. It was especially nice to have a place to stay in Washington, D.C. while the nation's bicentennial celebration was in full progress.

Since our visits were so infrequent, the relatives seemed as genuinely glad to see us as we were to see them. We tried to never stay any one place too long, though, because eight children, no matter how well behaved they are, do tend to fill up a house. May I also suggest a hostess gift is thoughtful and appropriate.

2. *We drove at night some of the time and saved a motel bill.* When we did this, we would check in at a motel the following noon and have an afternoon of relaxation by the pool or at local attractions. I would go to bed very early that night, while the children who had slept the previous night in the car watched television or played games. We never drove through two nights in a row.

3. *We ate only two meals a day.* Both of these would be hot, nutritious meals, usually during mid-morning and late afternoon. We ate in family restaurants, but there were certain things we never ordered. We never had dessert and we

never drank milk. Each day we would stop at a grocery store and get milk and sometimes cookies or fruit. Eight glasses of milk in a restaurant are costly; but eight paper cups and a half-gallon carton of milk are much less expensive.

4. *We looked for attractions with nominal or no admission charges.* This was very easy to do in Washington, D.C. with all its wonderful museums to visit. In New York City we did decide to splurge on a conducted tour of the city, which included a trip to the Statue of Liberty. In Philadelphia, Charleston, and St. Petersburg, we visited all the free historical sites. Williamsburg, on the other hand, was not one of our inexpensive days.

5. *We didn't buy souvenirs, except on rare occasions.* The children had a small allowance to spend as they wished; but cheap souvenirs were not high on their priority lists. I do remember small metal replicas of the Liberty Bell and the Statue of Liberty which came home with us.

After five weeks on the road I think we were all glad to get back home; but our experiences have never been forgotten. Even though fourteen years have passed since that summer, they still may say, "Hey, Mom, remember the time you broke your toe on the subway in New York City?" (How could I forget it? My son's big shoe hitting the end of my second toe and standing it up vertically as the train lurched to a stop is not a memory that soon fades.)

"We never had any money for a fancy vacation, but every year we took a trip. I had a big tent, and we'd go somewhere and camp out. It didn't matter where we'd go, just so long as we were all together and having fun." —DOLVA WATSON

Another voice then may be heard to say, "Do you remember when the car overheated in Washington, D.C. and the policeman let us park it on the grass parkway until it cooled down?" (I remember that time *and* the two other times it did the same thing in Philadelphia and Amarillo. My husband told me he had repaired that overheating problem!)

Another will ask "Do you remember when we locked the keys in the car when we went in that restaurant?" (I remember how three different people tried to help us before the fourth one finally arrived with a coat hanger. Whoever said New Yorkers aren't friendly?)

Our memories of family trips go on and on, and include the fun things, as well as the challenges. Once we learned how "easy" it was and how inexpensive we could make it, we continued to take other trips. While the 1976 bicentennial tour was probably our most memorable car trip, Jamaica was probably our best plane trip — although some of the kids might say Hawaii was. I particularly remember Jamaica, because that's where the entire family decided to go parasailing, and I was going along to sit on the beach and watch. (I'm afraid of heights.) But before I knew what was happening, the kids had convinced me that parasailing was something I shouldn't miss, and, after all, the eight children, a son-in-law, and my husband had already done it. I will never forget running on the beach, attached to the parachute, as the motorboat pulled me along. Before I knew it, I was leaving the ground, heading for the clouds. If I ever doubted my sanity, it was then. What in the world was a fifty-five-year-old woman, supposedly with good sense, doing flying around the sky? But I must say, I gained a lot of confidence from that journey. Once I landed safely on the ground and realized that I had made the ride without dying of a heart attack, I felt ten feet tall. I had done something that I had been afraid to do, and I had conquered my fear — well, for that day anyway. I haven't tried parasailing again.

Family vacations. What fun! What enjoyment! What memories! If you haven't enjoyed your children by spending a vacation with them, it is time to do it. Find the type of trip that suits your family best, and go for it. There will always be reasons why it isn't convenient; but don't let a few roadblocks stand in the way of a fantastic time for your family.

8

Being a Single Parent

"This is not the way my life was supposed to be," a young mother said as she shared her thoughts with others who belonged to the singles class at her church. "Not in my wildest dreams did I ever expect to be raising two children by myself and having to work at the same time. I didn't know life could be this difficult. It's like something that happens in the movies, something that happens to someone else—but never to you."

"I know what you mean," Tammy said. "It took me a year after my divorce to accept the fact that it really happened. I kept waiting to wake up from a bad dream. Then one morning, after months of crying, I finally said to myself, 'Life is not going to get any better if you don't look for ways to make it better.' From that point, life really has gotten better."

"If you think you had it bad, think how I felt," said Carl, a young father in his early thirties. "At least most of you women already knew how to take care of young children. When Carol was killed in the car accident, I didn't know how to do anything around the house. She had always stayed at home with Nikki and Elizabeth, and she'd taken care of everything. I had to learn to do even the simplest tasks."

"That must have really been tough," Milly said. "I think men and women each have different things to cope with when they become single parents; but the initial pain is there for all of us. At least being a man, you already had a good job and didn't have to worry about making enough money to live on. Unfortunately, statistics tell us that women just do not make the same money that men do, and usually we are the ones who are left to support the children."

"That reminds me of a seminar I attended not long ago," Tammy said. "The speaker was talking about divorce, and she said, 'When a man gets a divorce, he becomes single, but when a woman gets a divorce she becomes a single parent.'"

"That goes along exactly with what I read in a magazine," Milly added. "The article said that 95 percent of children in divorced homes live with their mothers. The ironic thing is that men keep their same standard of living, and women become poor."

"That may be true in some divorce cases, but it wasn't true in my situation," Carl said. "I couldn't keep my standard of living because I had to hire so many services. I don't think I truly appreciated all the things Carol did until I started looking for someone to take over some of the duties. I looked for a housekeeper who was willing to do housework, cook, care for the children, and also chauffeur them to their activities. I never found that person. I finally hired a housekeeper and then got someone else to care for the children. Believe me, that doesn't leave any money at the end of the month. After a year, I'm still not dating again, because frankly, I can't afford it."

"It's true, women don't usually have to provide the money for dates, so you'd think we could have a social life; but the fact is, most of us don't," Eunice said. "After we get home from work, we have all of our housework to do, and since we haven't seen the children all day, we want to spend time with them. Besides that, most of us can't afford to pay a baby-sitter, and it is rather awkward asking the date, before we accept the invitation, if he intends to take care of paying the sitter. I just can't do that."

"I'm too tired anyway," Tammy said. "Just having to think of adding one other thing to my life is more than I can handle. Maybe later when the girls are older I will have more energy."

"When my children were younger, I felt the same way that you do now," stated Molly, the oldest member of the class. "My entire life evolved around my children and my work. I didn't have time or energy for anything else. Now the children are in high school, and they are busy with their own activities. They see me sitting at home most of the time, and they encourage me to start dating again. But it is difficult for me now. I guess I've gotten rather set in my own ways of doing things, and I don't think I want to change. If I had it to do all over again, I'd make the effort to get out more from the very beginning."

"At the beginning of this discussion, I said my life had gotten better since I'd decided to do something about it," Tammy said. "What I actually mean is, I decided to start taking better care of myself. I certainly don't intend to neglect my children; but I can't live my life just for them. Anyway, they're the ones who profit from my taking care of myself, because then they are raised by a happier mother."

"Getting away from an abusive husband was my first step on the road to taking care of myself," Phyllis said. "I always believed that a marriage should last forever, and I particularly felt that way after children entered the home. So for years, I put up with my husband getting drunk and beating me; but when he started to beat the kids, I knew I had to leave. Since I don't have any entry-level work skills, I had to go on welfare. I used to be embarrassed about my circumstances, but I'm not any longer. I've prayed about it, and I now have some peace about what I've had to do. I realize that the children are much better off than they would have been in an abusive home, and I'm doing the best that I can to get my life in order. I start a new training program next week to learn how to be a checker at a grocery store."

Tammy, Milly, Carl, Molly, Eunice, and Phyllis are fortunate to be part of a singles group where they can share their fears, disappointments, concerns, and joys of being single parents. Many churches have recognized this growing need, and have provided classes and leaders for these singles, not only as a way to minister to their own parishioners, but also as a way to reach the unchurched.

"Being a parent wasn't easy when I was married, but it is doubly hard now that I'm single," said one young mother of two small children. "Making all the decisions alone is what is so hard for me. I just need to have someone to talk to, someone to reaffirm me, and tell me when I'm doing the right things. That is what this support group does for me. It keeps me from feeling so all alone."

Single mothers do feel alone some of the time. They describe themselves by using such words as penniless, tired, trapped, overworked, exhausted. However, some seem to have found ways to cope. Let's look at some of the issues and how these mothers have handled them:

Money

1. *Be honest with your children about your financial situation.* "There is just never enough," stated Melanie. "Once I recognized that fact, and stopped trying to fight it, I was better off. I have explained to the children that we can't have the same things that we had before. Instead of getting in a frenzy because I don't have money to take the children to McDonald's, I explain to them that the heating bill is up because we are having an exceptionally cold winter, and having heat in the house is more important than eating out. It is amazing how much more understanding the children are when I explain the real situation to them. Before, I'd just say, 'We can't go out because there is no money.' I think when we are honest as parents, and let the children know how bad it is at times, they feel more a part of the family and work better with us to handle the situation."

2. *Look for ways to bring more income into the family.*
"When I put the numbers on paper and saw how little money we actually had each month," said Theresa, "I knew I had to do something to generate more. My salary just wouldn't pay the existing bills, much less provide for anything new. I decided to go to the personnel department at the company where I worked and apply for whatever job was available that paid more money. For me, that was a bold act. I'm rather shy and usually I never ask for anything at work. There was an opening in a department which required working with computers, and ordinarily just the thought of learning something that new would have scared me to death. But because we needed the money so badly, I decided to take the risk. Fortunately for me and my family, I did, because knowing computers has opened the door for me twice since that time. In two years, I have nearly doubled my salary, and I still have room for advancement."

"A single mother does what she has to do. It's not always what she wants, and she may wish that it didn't have to be that way; but in order to reach a goal so she can make a better life for her children, she may have to accept help from someone else." —DOLVA WATSON

Sandra described her situation this way: "My children were teenagers when I became a single parent, and I knew I didn't have money to keep giving them their allowances. I called them all together one evening, and went over every step of the budget with them. I had to laugh even during that serious time when my fourteen-year-old son looked up with shock on his face, and said, 'But Mother, there is no money left for me.' The other two children, who were sixteen and seventeen at the time, had already come to that conclusion.

"So we decided to see what they could do to earn their own spending money. The seventeen-year-old got a job working at the grocery store after school. The sixteen-year-old worked in the local library, and the fourteen-year-old got the lawn mower out and started looking for jobs in the neighborhood. Actually, the fourteen-year-old ended up having more money than either of the other two. He even loaned me money some months when extra repairs were needed around the house. In retrospect, I see what a good learning experience it was for the children. They learned what it meant to live within a budget, and they also learned how to handle their own money."

3. *Scale down your standard of living.* "It's hard to change the way you've been living," Cynthia said. "I almost had a financial disaster before I learned not to reach for the same labels in the grocery store I was used to buying, and not to buy the children new clothes on the charge card. Instead of shopping at big department stores, I now go to discount houses."

"I have just cut down on my buying altogether," says Lil. "I buy only half the amount I used to, and I seem to get along just fine. I guess most of the things were luxuries that I used to think I couldn't live without. Now I buy only what my family really needs."

"I decided to sell the house after Bill died and move the family to something smaller," Evelyn said. "The children protested loudly, but I knew we didn't need and couldn't afford the upkeep of that big house. The house payment and the utility bills were reduced greatly when we moved, and I have never regretted my decision. A single mother has to face enough problems without adding financial worries that can be avoided."

4. *Save a little money each month for emergencies.* "When a friend told me I should save a little each month, I thought she was crazy," Terrie said. "How could I save when I didn't have enough to start with? I couldn't see how I could do it, until our washer broke and I didn't have the money to have it repaired. At that point, I took another look at the

budget, and made cuts in a couple of places. With money from those cuts, I saved a little each month until I had enough money to get the washer repaired. Now, wouldn't it have made more sense for me to have made those cuts earlier, saved the money, and had it in reserve when the washer broke down? Once I started saving just a little, I have never stopped; and I do not have the worry of not knowing what I'd do if an emergency came along. It's just one less thing I have to worry about."

5. *Continue to give your tithe to the Lord.* "When I first became a single parent, I thought, *Surely God doesn't expect me to tithe when I have so little,*" Connie said. "I had read about the widow's mite, but I didn't think that applied to me. I rationalized that God wanted me to have enough to take care of my children, and He wouldn't expect me to give during this period of my life. All during those months, my financial matters were in chaos. I just couldn't manage the little money I had. Finally, I said, 'All right, God, I can't do this alone. I need Your help. Please help me to get my finances in order.' And He did. I knew immediately that I needed to give my tithe first and let the other needs follow in their proper order. From that day until this, God has been faithful in helping me manage my finances. There has always been enough money each month to meet our needs."

"When women have a career, I feel they do not experience the empty-nest syndrome when their children leave home." —MARTHA SANFORD

Children

1. *Do not look to your children to fill your every need.* "I was lonely after my divorce, and I depended on my children to fill the void in my life," Monica said. "At first, they enjoyed all the attention I gave them; but it soon became

apparent that I was smothering them. When they wanted to both go away the same weekend to visit their father, I became frantic. What would I do all weekend by myself? At that point, I realized that I had to have a life outside of the time I spent with them. If I didn't, I would be emotionally crippled when they grew up and left home."

2. ***Do not overprotect your children.*** A mother of four speaks: "Because I thought I had to be both mother and father to my children after Jim's death, I became almost paranoid that I wasn't watching after them closely enough. After all, I reasoned, something had happened to Jim, and I had to make very certain that nothing happened to the kids. I wouldn't let them out of my sight other than when they were at school. My decisions were always imposed on them, because I couldn't take any chances on the inexperienced kids making a mistake. I soon came to realize I was doing the children a great disservice. By not allowing them to make decisions, I was sending the message that they were not to be trusted, that their opinions were not important, and that I wasn't interested in listening to them. The kids actually began to rebel in a variety of ways, and I knew I had to change what I was doing. I realized that being a single parent might give me the tendency to be overprotective, but I could not give in to being that way."

"One of the hardest things to do as a Christian mother is to put your faith and trust into action. It's so easy to say, 'Yes, Lord, I trust you.' But when difficult times come we have a tendency to take back that trust, and worry our way through the problem ourselves."
—Marlene Huffman

3. ***Let the children see you as a successful working mother.*** "There is no greater example I can be to my children than to let them see me going about my daily

life in a cheerful way," said the mother of two. "My daughters need to know that having a profession is important to a woman because no one ever knows when she may be called on to provide the living for the family. They also need to see me living by faith, one day at a time, and not unduly worrying about the future."

Yourself

1. *Single parents need to take care of their children's needs; but they also need to take care of their own.* The mother of two small children said, "When I first became a single parent, I worked so hard and worried so much that I became physically ill. It was at that time I realized that you can't take proper care of your children without taking care of yourself first. Now when I notice I am becoming stressed out or my energy is becoming low, I take a break. There is no one else to take care of the kids except me, and I must take very good care of my health, both physically and emotionally.

2. *Look for other people who are willing to help you, and don't hesitate to ask them.* "I was very hesitant to ask my parents to baby-sit when John and I broke up, because I felt like I made my bed and I should have to lie in it, so to speak," said Angie. "I didn't want anyone to help me, although many people offered, especially my parents. It wasn't until several months later that my sister asked me why I was punishing our parents. When I asked her what she was talking about, she said that my keeping the children away from Mom and Dad was causing them a lot of pain. I had not looked at it in that light. But then I realized that my pride of wanting to show everyone that I could do it all by myself was actually creating an unfair situation for my parents and my children."

Rita said, "I have volunteered in community service for several years; so when I became a single parent I was aware of many different resources available to my children and me. I enrolled the children in a YMCA swimming program, and

I joined an exercise class there, myself. I became active in a singles program at our church, and encouraged the boys to join the Tuesday-night basketball team. Being a single parent is a difficult job at best; but it is more bearable when other people are invited into our lives. Having an extended family is much better than being all alone.

    3. *Give of yourself to others.* These words were spoken by a young mother: "When I learned that Jack was not going to live, I felt angry and bitter. It wasn't fair that I should have to raise three children by myself. What had I ever done to deserve this? After Jack's death, I retreated into my own little world that included only the children and me. For over a year, I methodically went through each day, not allowing myself to be concerned about anything outside of my own family. Then one day I was reading the Bible and I came across Galatians 6:2. It says, 'Help each other with your troubles. When you do this, you truly obey the law of Christ.' I hadn't thought of helping anyone in over a year. All I had thought about was myself and my children. No wonder I had become such a miserable, unhappy person. Ever since that day, I have tried to find at least one person every week to help. It is amazing how much lighter our own burden becomes when we get busy helping someone else."

    No one has ever said that single parenting is easy; but some people seem to do it with grace and success. Many people look at it as only a temporary time in their lives, one which soon will be replaced by either marriage or the children's growing up. Most single mothers take it one day at a time and find that, with God's help, they are capable of raising well-adjusted and happy children.

9

Arranging Private Time for Mom

"What a difference! I actually feel like a human being again."

The glow on Jennifer's face spoke even more loudly than her words.

"You look fantastic, like you stepped off the cover of *Vogue*," said her friend Amy.

"I really had no idea what one day could do. And I don't even feel guilty about it!"

"Guilty? You shouldn't. You deserve a day like today. Now tell me all about it."

"I only have a minute. Jim and I are going out tonight; but I couldn't go home without stopping by so you could see the transformation."

"Take ten minutes and tell me about it," Amy encouraged. "I can't wait to hear. All I know is that Jim gave you this 'day of pampering' at Neiman Marcus for your anniversary."

"Like I said before, I can't believe that Jim ever came up with such a creative idea. He usually just sends flowers for our anniversary; but I guess he wanted to make it more special because it's our fifth."

"I personally think Jim should get the 'Husband of the Year' award. If Sam ever did anything like this for me, I'd be the happiest woman in the world."

"Maybe he will. I never thought Jim would do it. I've never been more surprised in my life than I was last night when he told me I had a ten o'clock appointment this morning, and he planned to stay home and keep the kids so I could be away all day."

"He even gave up his Saturday golf?"

"That's right. Even his golf."

"Wow! He does deserve that award."

"That's not all. He knows how much I like to get all dressed up and go out to dinner, so he arranged for a sitter and we're going out at seven."

"Well, all you have to do is slip into a dress. Your hair and face are already perfect. What else did you have done?"

"You can't see them, but my toes have just experienced their very first professional pedicure. My toenails are painted passion pink!" Taking a moment to observe Amy's look of delight, she continued, "Besides the obvious—the haircut, shampoo and style, facial and makeup, and manicure—I also received a body massage that relaxed every muscle in my body. And at lunch time, they served a delicious hot lunch from the Zodiac Room."

"It sounds perfectly wonderful."

"It was. I've never had a day all to myself since before Carrie arrived four years ago, and especially not since Matthew got here. There just isn't time for me to think of myself."

"Yeah, I know what you mean," Amy said soberly. After a pause, she said it again, almost inaudibly. "I do know what you mean."

Probably most young mothers can relate to Amy's reply. There just doesn't seem to be time for Mom to do anything for herself. All week she takes care of the house, her husband, the kids, the dog, and sometimes her away-from-home job; then she feels guilty if she sneaks out for a manicure on Saturday because she thinks she should be spending every minute with her family when she can be at home.

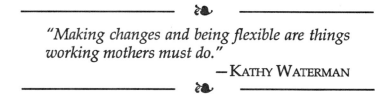

"Making changes and being flexible are things working mothers must do."
— KATHY WATERMAN

If she is truly going to be a happy parent who enjoys her family and her life, there are a few basic rules a mother should observe:

1. ***Schedule an appointed hour or two each week which is "Mommy's time."*** It doesn't mean spending money. Not too many mothers can have an entire day of pampering like Jennifer had. But I discovered through the years that unless it is designated in advance, the available time will be taken up doing something else.

What the mother does with her time will depend on what brings her the most relaxation and joy. One young mother told me that she feels pretty all week if she can just have one hour to get her nails manicured. The mother of a small baby said if she could get out for one luncheon a week and have adult conversation with a friend, she was happy, while another mother wanted some type of physical activity. She said she really didn't miss shopping for herself, or luncheons, or beauty appointments; but she did miss her hour of running every day. When a friend asked her if she didn't get enough running by just chasing a two- and four-year-old around the house every day, she laughed and responded, "There is a difference! My hour of running gives me complete solitude. That is what I miss the most—solitude." Another mother said she needed an hour a day when she first got home from work to just unwind before she felt ready to start handling problems at home.

All of these are legitimate needs, and a way should be worked out so the mother can have them met. The woman who gives continuously without having her own needs met is setting herself up for resentment. Sometime in the future, she will feel angry that everyone else is being taken care of, and she isn't. She may continue to serve her family, but the joy will be gone. It is much easier to recognize that everyone—yes, even the all-sacrificing mother—needs some time just for herself; she should not pretend that she doesn't.

2. *Share the workload.* While the home and the children may have been previous mothers' private domains where no one else helped, the mother today will find she is much happier, and her family is, too, if the home becomes "ours" instead of "mine." Work should be shared with her husband, and also with each child, depending on his or her age.

In earlier times, children worked alongside their parents in the fields, in shops, and in the home. It has just been within the last few generations that children have not had to share in the family's work. Of course there are always exceptions. Some parents feel their children gain a sense of self-worth by having duties to share around the home.

How the work is divided among the children will be up to each individual household. One mother may feel that requiring a seven-year-old to make his own bed, pick up his room, and take out the trash is enough. Another mother may want her seven-year-old to do those things as well as help in the kitchen. Judy, a mother of an eight-year-old, said she purposefully assigned her daughter chores which would be done in the same room Judy was working in. She believed they would be missing valuable time together if they were working in two separate rooms.

Many mothers have expressed frustration about children helping around the house. They say that the work is not done exactly as they would like to have it done, and it is easier to do it themselves. When asked a more direct question—Is it the quality of work done or the time it takes the child to do it?—they usually say it is the latter. Too often mothers think it is easier to do a task quickly themselves than to supervise the learning process. While it is true that children work slower in the beginning when they are learning a task, they will be more efficient as time goes by. Practice usually increases speed, as well as perfection. The extra time a mother takes in the beginning will usually pay dividends in the years to come.

Some grocery stores now have small shopping carts for children to push around while they are in the store with their parents. They have found that mothers help the children select things to put in the smaller cart—and, happily for the store, the woman ends up buying more. While this may be a way for the store to raise its profits, it is also a way of teaching a young child how to buy groceries. When children who have had this experience are older, they will know what to look for when taking things off the grocery shelf.

The most efficiently run households seem to be those which have been well organized from the beginning. To avoid any confusion as to which chores are assigned to each family member, a large calendar is posted on the refrigerator door in many homes. The chores are written on the calendar, and regularly rotated to avoid boredom. Necessary supplies for doing the chores are kept in a designated place familiar to each person. When someone uses the last of any supply, that person is responsible for adding it to the grocery list, which is also posted on the refrigerator. A family meeting is held each month to discuss which chores are the most time consuming and to brainstorm different ways of streamlining that task. One teenager was delighted to find by changing brands of silver polish, her polishing time was cut in half.

When women today are asked what they need most, they usually say more household help, and studies have shown that women who receive the most help seem to experience the least amount of stress. All of this help need not come from the children alone. The husband should also be involved. And, like the children, he may need some training. Mary, a working mother of three, said, "Not all men come into a marriage knowing how to do household chores. I know mine didn't."

Many a husband gets to sit in front of the television at night while his wife rushes from one task to another simply because he doesn't know "how" to help. One young husband and father took exception to that premise and said, "If my wife would tell me what she wants me to do and then *show* me how to do it, I'd be glad to help." Instead of becoming frustrated because her husband isn't helping, a mother may simply need to take the time to lay out a schedule of work she would like him to do, and then help him, the first few times, to do it.

Here are other ways to get more help from Dad:

• *Make out the chore list with Dad's interests in mind.* Bob's mother did not require chores of him when he was growing up, so he came into a marriage with no experience in this area. As a result, Linda did all the household work, as well as her nine-to-five job—until after Jamie was born. When her maternity leave was up and it was time to go back to her job, she immediately realized that she could no longer handle everything by herself. Doing the usual household work, along with the new duties of washing all the baby clothes, making formula, bathing Jamie and putting her to bed, then getting up with her at least once during the night became an impossible assignment. At the end of the first week, Linda was exhausted. Realizing something had to be done, she and Bob sat down and made a list of things he would do.

Two weeks later, feeling proud of his accomplishments, Bob said to a friend, "Housework isn't nearly as bad as most men make it out to be. Of course, I did get to pick and choose what I wanted to do. I don't mind doing the grocery shopping if Linda gives me a detailed list, and vacuuming and running a washer of clothes are no big deal. I'm even getting to know Jamie better by getting up with her every other night. But thank goodness, Linda didn't give me kitchen duty. I really hate those dishes."

While some mothers may say it is unfair for husbands to pick what they like and let the woman do what is left, she should be reminded that having a happy husband helping with the chores is better than having no help or having a resentful husband who has to be constantly reminded to do the chores which he hates. And if there is a chore that both husband and wife hate equally, that chore may be shared on a rotating basis.

• *Spell out in detail how you want your husband to perform his tasks.* Judy complained that she hated for her husband to make the beds because he didn't square off the corners of the sheets. Being a nurse, this skill was something Judy had learned in nursing school. When she was reminded that Frank had neither been in the service or to nursing school, and when he had an opportunity to learn the "correct" way of making a bed, the problem was soon solved. Frank now squares off his corners as well as anyone. Similarly, Gloria complained that her husband brought the less expensive brands of canned goods when he shopped at the grocery store. When she started including the name brands on her list and explained to Rob why she thought those brands were preferable, her pantry then held the labels she preferred.

"Men are task oriented. Women need to target their home-care needs to their husbands for maximum cooperation." —BONNIE BEAR

• *Talk to your husband about how he feels his chores are working out.* He might appreciate some minor adjustments but hesitates to say anything in fear it will look like he is complaining. If communication is kept open, frustration will not have an opportunity to build to the boiling point at some later time.

- *Let your husband know how important his contributions are.* You might make him aware of the study done by Dr. Candice Feiring of the Educational Testing Service in Princeton. This study shows that the sense of support and validation a woman feels when her husband helps with the chores transfers directly into her mothering. Dr. Feiring found that the more support a man provides, the more sensitive his wife's behavior will be with their sons and daughters.
- *Let your husband and children know they are appreciated.* No one likes to work without getting some recognition. The positive stroke may come in the form of a simple statement, or it may be something more elaborate. One family decided to celebrate each weekend if their jobs were done well all week. If one child was lagging behind in his or her chores, peer pressure was applied by the others to get the job done so the celebration would not be canceled. How elaborate the celebration is depends on the family budget. One family might order pizza to be brought in while another group might all go out to dinner in a nice restaurant. The main thing to keep in mind is to show appreciation in some way.

3. *Don't feel guilty.* Guilt seems to be a word that comes up frequently when mothers get together. Some feel guilty if they work outside the home; others feel guilty if they do not. Some feel guilty about leaving their children in a daycare center; others feel guilty if they are at home all day and their children do not come in contact with other children. The list goes on and on. No matter what situation the mother is in she can usually find something to feel guilty about if she allows herself to. She needs to realize that feeling guilty takes energy which can be better used in more constructive ways.

"It's easy just to say, 'Don't feel guilty,' but it is a lot harder to really do it," said Janice, a young mother of four. Her friend Kelly agreed with her; but Kelly said she had been working on her guilt and she had made strides in reducing it. Maybe you can, too.

Ask yourself the following questions:
- *Why do I feel guilty?* Find out if you have a legitimate reason, and if you do, look at ways to correct the situation. Mary felt guilty that her family ate so much fast food which she picked up regularly on the way home from work. She found that her food bill went down, as well as her guilt level, when she decided to plan a menu a week in advance and stick to it. By doing some of the food preparation before she left home in the morning, she found that the time required in the evening to complete the meal was minimal.

If you are trying to be a super-mom and feel guilty when you find that is impossible, take another look at your expectations. Focus on all the things you do get done in a week, not on the things you have not accomplished. Ask yourself if it is really reasonable to think you can do more than you are already doing.
- *How can I simplify my life, so I won't feel guilty?* One mother was amazed at how much better she felt when she removed the clutter from her home. She had felt guilty because her house never looked like she wanted it to. As hard as she worked to keep it clean, she thought it was never quite up to par. Friends, dropping in unannounced, added to her embarrassment. One Saturday she enlisted the help of her husband and children, and all items in the house which were not essential or had not been used in the last six months were boxed and put in the basement or given away. Without the clutter, the entire family could find things more readily, and each room stayed tidy. Then, by doing the same amount of work each week, the house remained orderly and the mother no longer felt guilty about how it looked.
- *What adjustments can I make in my life to avoid the guilt I feel?* Louise felt guilty because she was not spending the amount of time with her daughter that she thought she should. She looked at her schedule and found she could change some of her activities. Instead

of spending Thursday night at choir practice, she decided to enroll in a mother-daughter craft night that met every Friday at the church. Instead of dropping her daughter off at ballet class, Louise decided to stay and watch the lesson, at least every other time. She tried to take along any handwork, such as lowering a hem in a dress, so she could accomplish another task while she was waiting.

4. *Hire help, if at all possible.* "I could never do that," Wanda replied. "I'd feel so guilty if I used some of the family budget to get household help." There's that word again, guilt. Wanda was the mother of four children, a certified public accountant, an active church member, and a leader in her community. Yet she would feel guilty if she hired a cleaning lady once a week! On the other hand, Joy has a less demanding job, and only two children, but she has household help once a week and also sends her husband's shirts out to be laundered. She doesn't hide her feelings when she states, "Time is money, and my time is valuable. I'd rather trim the budget in other areas than spend an entire evening ironing shirts."

Hiring a baby-sitter also comes under this category, especially if the mother is at home all day. It may be for only two hours a week, but that will be a time the mother can look forward to each week when she can have a little time for herself. If the mother works away from home, she will still want to have a sitter occasionally so she and her husband can get away for an evening together.

When our children were young, I was fortunate to find a little, gray-haired lady down our street who was a retired kindergarten teacher. Her name was Mrs. Gunderson, but all the children on the block called her Gunny. We had five children when we first moved to that house, and when I asked a neighbor to recommend a baby-sitter, she immediately told me about Gunny, whom she had used when her children were younger. With some hesitation, I dialed Gunny's number, a little fearful she might say no when she heard I had five children. Quite the contrary, she said she could handle five just fine—and Gunny certainly could! Within a few years, she was sitting for our eight.

She always arrived at our house with an armload of books which she checked out weekly at the library. The children loved to crawl up in her lap or sit at her side, and hear the characters come to life as only Gunny could make them. If she were baby-sitting in the afternoon, she might take the children to the park or to the train station to see the train come in, or to her house where she kept a menagerie of animals. If a bird ever fell out of a nest or any animal was injured, the children on the block immediately took it to Gunny's house, because she knew just what to do.

On each child's birthday, Gunny invited that person to her house for breakfast. She lived in a small cottage behind another house, and although it was modest by most standards, her home was filled with warmth and love. For the birthday celebration she always made that child's favorite dishes, served on her best china. Baking a special coffee cake or preparing a delicious omelet never seemed to be too much trouble for her.

Gunny is no longer living. She died at age eighty-two when she was struck by a car as she crossed a busy street, on her way to baby-sit some other children a few blocks away. Not having a car, Gunny always walked to church, to concerts, to the grocery store, or wherever she needed to go. She was really quite a walker. I was amazed when she told me the story of how, when she was younger, she had walked from her home in South Dakota to California. She was really a remarkable lady.

Over the twelve-year period that Gunny was a part of our family's life, she contributed greatly to our happiness. She provided me the opportunity to have some mornings or evenings free to do things I enjoyed, and she enriched the lives of the children in countless ways.

I often think how different all of our lives would have been if I had not looked for a baby-sitter. If I had thought I could do it all by myself, I certainly would have been cheating my children of some wonderful experiences. Sometimes when a mother helps herself, her children turn out to be the winners.

5. *Look for services in your community.* Some churches have mother's-day-out programs. One morning a week mothers may leave their children at the church, where they will be cared for by qualified childcare providers. Many mothers have found this to be one of the most important ministries the church provides for them. One mother summed it up by saying, "Because of mother's day out, I am able to keep my sanity."

Some libraries have children's story hour. Having the child participate in this activity allows the mother time to enjoy reading her own favorite book while her child is in another room hearing a story.

The YMCA often provides numerous activities for children. An afternoon of swimming lessons or field trips provided by qualified personnel may give Mom a much-needed break.

A stop at your local Chamber of Commerce may provide you with a list of other activities in your community. Take advantage of some of these services—and don't feel guilty about it.

6. *Now and then, arrange a weekend away from home.* The mother may want to go away with her husband at one time, and she may want to go by herself at another. While making the arrangements to leave and actually getting away is sometimes time consuming, most mothers will agree that it is well worth the effort.

These weekend trips need not be expensive. A camping trip with your husband may be something both of you would enjoy. Or if you want something which involves less work on your part, you may want to travel to a nearby city and get a moderately priced hotel for two nights. Weekends are a great time to get special rates at some of the more expensive hotels. Some of these hotel specials include a continental breakfast and discount tickets to local entertainment. Some of the newer "suite" hotels have kitchens, so you may want to take food from home, and thus only have the expense of the room. Even if you do not have money for the theater or fancy restaurants, just the fact that you have a change of scenery and time to spend with your husband will make the trip worthwhile. A moonlight stroll along a beach or a tree-lined street can often give a couple the needed time to help strengthen a marriage.

On the weekends when you want to get away by yourself, you might visit a friend. I have a good friend in Northern California, and when our children were small, she and I used to visit each other at least once a year. We'd leave the children with our husbands and have a delightful day shopping in San Francisco or Los Angeles. Both our husbands were engineers who traveled frequently, leaving us with total care of the children; therefore, neither of us felt guilty when we took these weekend excursions, which soon came to be known as our "business trips." Two days away from the children gave us both new appreciation for them, and them for us.

Whether you take weekend trips or day trips, just remember that you deserve to have some time away from your children. You are not being a bad mother in leaving them. To the contrary, you are probably becoming a better mother, because by taking care of yourself, you are more able to take care of them. And you can certainly enjoy them a lot more.

10

Using "Never" and "Always"

Mothers are often told never to say "never," and never to say "always." While this may be true most of the time, I think there are exceptions to the rule. I believe a Christian mom will find consistency a valuable tool in raising her children, and consistency means there will be some things which she will *never* do and other things which she will *always* do. As a result, her children will know that she will be unwavering on certain things, and they will feel a sense of support and safety from this structure. Let's look at some of those situations.

1. *A mom should never, never give up on her children.* In the years I worked with teenagers as a high-school counselor, I saw all kinds of injustices done by parents who were at the end their ropes, did not know what to do, and simply gave up their parenting duties. I saw high-school students kicked out of their homes and locks changed on the doors before they could return to get clothes to wear to school. I saw a boy sleeping on a football field because he didn't have anywhere else to go after his parents told him never to return. I witnessed young ladies being called all kinds of names by their moms—names which would cause any girl to doubt her sense of worth. I saw kids whose

mothers were too busy with their own lives to be bothered with what was happening to their sons and daughters. Too often, these parents were ready to either put their children out on the street to grapple for themselves or to give their parenting duties to anyone else who would step in and try to help.

When I saw these situations, I often thought of the words Jesus said to His followers, " . . . You can be sure that I will be with you always. I will continue with you until the end of the world" (Matt. 28:20). What a reassuring promise we have that Jesus is with us always, through good times and bad times. If Jesus is truly our example, then how can we as parents not stand by our children through periods of painful disappointment, disillusionment, and disobedience? This does not mean that we do not continue to discipline them, or that we let them get away with "murder"; but it does mean that young people will always know that a parent is standing by them, no matter what happens. "Standing by" may mean simply standing firm. It may involve taking action which is not always easy, such as placing a drug abuser in a rehabilitation center. But it also means that a young person will know beyond a shadow of a doubt that the parents are praying for him or her and that their support is constant and unyielding.

A professional football player tells the story of how he grew up without a father and how he ran with a bad crowd all during high school and college. After he joined the professional team, he continued to get in one scrape after another, until finally he was suspended. Some years later, he turned to God and got his life in order. As he told his story to young people across the nation, he always remembered to make one point. He said, "No matter what I was doing bad, or how far I strayed, I knew that my mother still loved me and was at home praying for me. Knowing that she had not given up on me was what finally convinced me to do something about my life."

A high-school boy named Tom was reared in a Christian home by a loving father and mother. But during his teenage years he began to rebel against the values he had been taught, acting out in ways the mother and father never thought possible. Finally, his breaking curfew, drinking, failing in school, and threatening to run away drove his father to say, "Let him leave if he wants to. I've had enough." But the mother said, "No. I will never give up on Tom. We must keep working until we find a way to help him." Professional counseling was obtained, and Tom began to sort through the reasons for his actions. He later confessed to his parents that in his confused state of mind, he was trying to see how far he could go before they would stop loving him. He had always known he'd been adopted as a baby, and during the teenage years he began to wonder if his birth mother had really loved him—and for that matter, if his adoptive parents did. By standing strong, the parents helped Tom get through his troubled times. The following year, he made all A's in school and went on to college and a career.

2. *A mom should always let her children know she has time for them.* Most mothers would say, "Of course, I have time for my children." But often this is not true. Mothers may be at home all day and not have time for their children because they are involved in their own worlds, which may include their own hobbies, volunteer projects, or household duties. Working mothers may not have time for their children because they have not set their priorities in order and have too many other things to do.

"It is not a matter of working or not working. It's a matter of establishing proper priorities. My first priority must be God; the second is my husband; the third is my children; and work comes after that." —MARLENE HUFFMAN

Sylvia lived in a beautiful home with a successful dad and a busy, civic-minded mom. While she certainly had all the material things anyone else in her high school had, she didn't seem happy. One day while talking to a friend she said, "I wish I had brothers and sisters like you do. It must be nice to have someone at home to talk to." When her friend asked what she meant, Sylvia answered that she was alone most of the time. Her father's job demanded long hours and extensive travel, and her mother, avoiding the loneliness of being home alone while Sylvia was at school, had become more and more involved in fund drives and other community work that also kept her away from home at night. While these parents thought they were giving their daughter "everything," they failed to see what she needed most was their time.

Nancy was a working mother who believed in running her life like a drill sergeant would run a platoon. Everything had a time and place, and her schedule would not be bent. Because she appeared so efficient, and her life seemed so well organized, she was admired by her co-workers, who saw her as a very successful career person, always in control. When she left work and started her duties at home, she continued her same mode of operation. Her three children knew what they had to do, and they did it. The house was immaculate. The only problem was that Nancy ran everything on such a tight schedule she did not allow time to really be with her children. They were all in the house together, but Mom was more concerned about the order of things than she was about what her children were thinking or feeling.

Having time for your children means more than just being available to attend their school events or sporting games. It means being able to sit down and listen to them, to let them know you are truly interested in what they have to say and what is happening in their lives.

Having time for a child's special interest when he or she is young may even influence their choice of a major in college. My oldest daughter, Alissa, wanted to take piano lessons when she was only four years old. I had decided to take lessons strictly as a hobby, and she would climb up on the piano bench and watch me practice. Soon she was wanting to do what I was doing. When I told my piano teacher about my daughter's interest, she recommended a teacher in a nearby city who specialized in very young children. Then, every week, Alissa, her two younger brothers, their six-month-old sister, and I would drive to the nearby city for the lesson. Daily, I would sit on the piano bench with my daughter as she practiced. We counted out each measure of music together. Before long, I gave up my lessons; but Alissa continued hers. She majored in music in college and now is actively involved in the music program of her church. I have never resumed my lessons, but I still have my John Thompson's third grade book in case I need it later on.

3. *A mom should never let her job become her god.* Felice Schwartz, author of the "mommy track" article in *Harvard Business Review*, states unequivocally, "If a woman really wants to make it to the highest levels of the corporation, then she cannot be a primary player in her children's lives." Yet we see mothers who are trying to do just that. They were high achievers in college and are still working under the premise they can reach any goal if they work hard enough. They are the moms who believe they can truly have it all — and if they find they can't, they think they have failed.

"I have always considered my husband and the children my career, and nursing my profession. What I mean is my husband and children are my number-one priority, but when I walk out the door to go on duty, I give my full attention to my profession." — ANN BENGFORD

There is a difference between being a working mom and being a woman so driven to succeed on her job that she puts her career above her husband and children. Probably very few women actually intend to fall into this latter category; but they get all caught up in their own successes. One promotion leads to another with each new job description requiring a little more time and effort.

LaVerne had worked as a contract assistant in an engineering firm before her first child was born. Her job was interesting but nothing she really minded leaving. She enjoyed staying at home with her two children until they started school, but at that point she thought she should help contribute to the family income. Getting a job at her former place of employment wasn't difficult because the company was experiencing great strides of growth, and before long, LaVerne was on the fast track of success. As some people would say, "she was at the right place at the right time." She was first promoted from the job of assistant and later she was made contracts manager of her department. As the years went by and the company continued to grow, LaVerne continued to get one promotion after another. By the time her children were in high school, she was in charge of contracts for the entire company. She knew her job took priority in her life, but she rationalized that she was actually doing it for the children. After all, she was now making much more money than her husband, who was a teacher, and because of her salary they would be able to send the two children to the finest colleges.

I met this woman when her children were in their junior and senior years in high school; the distraught person weeping in my counseling office was hardly the picture one would have of a tough-minded contract negotiator. For over an hour I listened while she poured out the pain of her broken heart to me. We had scheduled her appointment to talk about the decline in both of her children's grades and their apparent truancies from school; but she was too emotionally upset to dwell on those things that morning. The night before her husband had told her he wanted a divorce—he had found someone else.

I will never forget her words as she said, "I knew better than to let my job become my god. I just got caught up in my own success and didn't have time for my husband and children."

A working mom may have to turn down certain promotions until later in her life when such a change will not jeopardize her role as a mother. While this may be difficult for success-minded women, the cost of deciding otherwise may be too great.

4. *A mom should never think her children are too busy with their own school activities to need her.* When I hear a mom say her children are so involved in their world that they don't need her, I find that I am hearing an alibi for the mother's own lack of time. While it is true that older youngsters do become very involved in school activities, and they seem constantly to be on the go, they still need to know Mom is there for them when they do want to talk.

High school is the time when peers become so important to young people, and parents often feel threatened by this outside influence. It is also a time when adolescents are searching for ways to be more independent. When teenagers do not spend as much time or share as many happenings with the parents as they did the year previously, the parents often take this as a sign that their children no longer need them. Some parents find this to be a very troubling time, because they may feel rejected and lonely. Other parents who are anxious to complete their parenting years gladly welcome this new period, and may even pull farther away from the children.

While young people certainly need to be given more freedom during the adolescent years to develop and grow, they also need to feel the strong support of a parent who is there for them when things go wrong. One mother had been invited to school on several occasions to talk to the counselor about discipline problems her son was having. No one incident was major, but minor infractions of rules seemed to plague this young man. Mischief seemed always to twinkle in his eye.

The mother was always firm with her son, letting him know when she did not approve of his behavior; but at the same time, she showed a positive approach in her dealings with him. One day when she stopped by the school to visit, when he wasn't in trouble, she confided to me that she was happy he was going through these problems while he was still in high school. When I gave her a quizzical look, she explained, "I had a friend whose son was perfect in high school, but when he got to college he got into all kinds of negative things. I'm glad my son is learning his lessons, as painful as they may be, while I am here to support him."

"When children are teenagers, it is so important to help them look the very best they can, whether that means getting braces on the teeth, going to the dermatologist, styling the hair, or buying clothes. Some people think this is shallow, but teenagers need to really feel good about themselves. Looking good helps them to feel good."
—JOAN PENNINGTON

No matter what signals you may think you are receiving from a son or daughter, do not feel that you are no longer needed. True, the need may be a different kind; but it is still present. Instead of being in the forefront, you may be more in the background, where you may need to talk less and listen more. As one mother put it, "Donna doesn't need me to drive her around any longer or help her decide which dress to wear; but she does need me to listen when she wants to talk."

5. *A mom should always keep her commitments to her children, even if it means sacrificing something important to her.* As busy as today's mothers are, keeping commitments to their children can sometimes be difficult. "When I promised Marla I'd take her to the zoo on Saturday, I had forgotten I had this big project due on my boss's desk Monday morning," a young woman said. "Sometimes I just feel so torn. I want to keep my promises, but what am I to do?"

If children are to grow up knowing their moms mean what they say, then those moms must follow through on their commitments. "But Darrin always understands when something comes up and I can't take him to the place we'd planned to go," Fern stated. When Darrin was asked how he felt about not getting to go to the Dodgers game with his mom, his reply was, "It's no big deal. I didn't think I'd get to go anyway. Something always comes up to keep us from going places."

Mothers need to plan ahead sufficiently to know when conflicts may arise. If their work does not allow them to do this, then maybe they should not make plans with their children until closer to the appointed date. If the event is scheduled months in advance, like a school Christmas program, then Mom should not let anything else, except a true emergency, keep her from that commitment. One single parent laughingly asked, "Not even a date with a good-looking man?"

No, not even a date with Prince Charming, himself.

6. *A mom should always share the family chores with her children.* Being part of a group is very important to people, especially to children. Gangs have increased their membership because kids want to feel accepted and to feel they belong. Families can give this feeling of belonging if each person is seen as an important, contributing member. This does not mean that a child must have a long chore list in order to feel like he or she belongs to the family; but it does mean the duties, no matter how small they may be, need to be appreciated. Family members who work together, help each other, and share the chores will have an appreciation for each other and for themselves.

7. *A mom should never "put down" her children in front of their teachers, friends, or siblings.* Bill was a quiet, unassuming young man. I knew him only slightly because he was not one to visit a counseling office frequently. There was a certain angelic look about this boy that was both appealing and disarming. He was a good student, and I had never heard anyone on campus speak badly of him. No one could have been more surprised than I was when his mother called for an appointment to speak to me about "problems" Bill was having.

When Bill and his mother entered my office, the mother started to talk immediately. "I can't believe this lazy son of mine has let his chemistry grade drop from an A to a B," she said without any prior greeting. The report cards would not be out for a few more weeks, so I really wasn't sure what she was referring to. Before I could ask, she continued, "He had a test last week and he made a B simply because he did not study. I told him that he's turning out just like his no-good, bum father. That man was brilliant, but he was as lazy as they come. I left him when Bill was a baby because I couldn't stand his sitting around the house all day, just too lazy to make anything of himself."

"Mothers need to relax and not be uptight. Believe in your children, and expect them to follow the rules." — BONNIE BEAR

Bill was sitting with his eyes cast down toward the floor. As I started to say something, she interrupted me and continued. "This kid doesn't have to do anything except make good grades. He doesn't have to work at an after-school job. He doesn't even have to help at home. All I ask of him is that he make good grades so he can become somebody—you know, someone important. But if he continues like he is going, he might as well just quit right now," she said.

I glanced at Bill, and my heart went out to him. I turned to the lady who was belittling her son, and said, "but Bill is already someone important. He is important to me and to a lot of people on this campus."

The mother calmed down, and we began to talk with Bill about ways he could work to bring his grade back up to an A before report-card time. After their appointment was over, and I was alone in my office, I reflected back on that conversation. How could any mother be so insensitive to her child? How could she put him down like that in front of another person? I was confident that Bill would have brought his grade back up anyway, but I wasn't nearly as confident that his self-esteem would remain at a high level.

Well-meaning parents sometimes try to help their children in a way that is very destructive. Bill's mother had taken time off from work because she was concerned about her son's grade. Her intentions were good, but her approach to the problem was both insensitive and harmful.

Christian mothers and fathers should heed Colossians 3:21: "Fathers, do not nag your children. If you are too hard to please, they may want to stop trying."

8. *A mom always builds self-esteem by using honest praise.* Dr. Wayne Dyer said, "Once you see a child's self-image begin to improve, you will see significant gains in achievement areas, but even more important you will see a child who is beginning to enjoy life more."

Mom and Dad are the most important persons in a very young child's life, and how much love and praise that child receives from these two people will be instrumental in how that child feels about himself or herself. One mother was asked how many times a day she bestowed praise on her two-year-old. She thought for a moment and then said, "I wish you'd asked me that question a year ago. Then I was always saying such things as, 'What a good boy you are.' But this year I think all I ever say is 'No, you can't do that.'" While every mother can relate to the "terrible two's," even during this trying period, mothers need to look for good things that the child does and praise him or her as often as possible.

This honest praise should continue throughout the child's life. Make a mental note to notice when a son or daughter is doing something right and give praise at that moment.

When the mother of a high-school girl was asked how often she praised her daughter her comment was, "Oh, she knows how great I think she is. I don't have to tell her." That comment should be filed in the same box as the one from the husband who says he doesn't have to tell his wife that he loves her because she already knows it. No matter how much someone may know they are loved and appreciated, hearing the words is still very important.

9. *A mother should always answer questions about her work when her children ask.* "How many people work in your office?" seven-year-old Crystal wanted to know after her mother's first day on the job.

"About ten," Mrs. Berry answered as she hurried with the dinner preparations.

"Are they nice?" Crystal asked.

"Yes, they seem to be."

"What do they do in the office?" the questioning continued.

"All kinds of different jobs," Mrs. Berry responded.

"Like what?" Crystal probed.

"Typing, answering the phone, putting information into the computers—things like that."

"Is that what you do?"

"Not all of those things."

"Well, what do you do?"

"Crystal, could we please talk about my job later? I really do have to get dinner now. Why don't you go in and watch television?"

Mothers often want to forget their jobs when they come home. They don't want to think about them again until the next morning, especially if the day has been pressured and nerve-racking. After all, they think, just a little peace and quiet shouldn't be too much to ask for, should it?

Again, I think of mothers who have sat in my counseling office complaining about not knowing what is going on in their children's lives. The usual comment is that the son or daughter "never tells me a thing." Frequently I asked those mothers how much of their own lives they share with their sons or daughters. Did the mother tell the child about her workday? What kind of a role model was she to her child?

Young children are inquisitive about what Mommy is doing, and no matter how tired or rushed Mommy is, she should always answer questions about her work. The unknown world of her work may be frightening to the child, and if he or she finds Mommy willing to talk about it in a pleasant way, those fears may be alleviated.

10. *A mom should never talk about her world when her children are trying to tell her about theirs.* How often we hear of children trying to explain a difficult problem they are having in school, only to have the parent come back with the words, "That's nothing. You should hear how rough I had it in school." Then the parent proceeds to recall incident after incident of past school days. By the time the parent is finished talking, the child is completely out of the mood to relay any further experience he or she may have had.

The same is often true of the working mother. Eleven-year-old Melody was waiting anxiously for her mother to come home from work. She had made a new friend at school, a new girl who had enrolled in her class that same day. It had been difficult for Melody the past few months with her dad and mom separating. She had moved with her mom to her grandmother's home, and leaving all her friends behind had been hard. It was especially disappointing when she found the children in her new class had already paired off into sets of "best friends," and she really had no one. The new girl arriving today was just the break she'd been hoping for.

"Mom, is that you?" Melody called out as she heard the front door open.

"It's me," Mrs. Peters responded as she dropped an armload of work on the entryway table.

"Mom, I have some of the most exciting news to tell you," Melody said as she sprang from the couch.

"And, I have some wonderful news to tell you," Mrs. Peters echoed.

"A new girl moved into town and she is in my class," Melody said hurriedly.

"That's wonderful, dear. Now let me tell you about a new advertising account I landed today. This could really mean I now have job security. You can't imagine how I've worried about supporting the two of us."

"This girl's name is Rhonda, and she has red hair and funny-looking freckles on her nose. And she is real friendly."

"How nice," Mrs. Peters answered with little apparent interest. Reverting the conversation back to herself, she said, "Mr. Harvey called me into his office, and told me how pleased he was with what I had been able to accomplish in such a short time. He said this was an account he's hoped his agency would get one day." As a smile of satisfaction came over her face, she continued, "but he said he didn't think a new person would be the one to bring it in."

"I'm proud of you, Mom," Melody injected. "The new girl lives just a couple of blocks away."

Apparently hearing only the first remark, Mrs. Peters said, "Well, I'm rather proud of myself, also. Mr. Harvey went on to ask me how I did it. He wanted to hear what strategies I used and if I'd found them to be successful in the past. He even wanted to discuss future accounts he thought I should go after. Isn't that just wonderful!"

"Yes, Mom. It's wonderful. Come on, let's eat. Grandma has it all ready." Melody had given up trying to share the news she had so eagerly wanted to tell her mother.

While it is important to share news as a family, a working mother needs to be sensitive to her son or daughter when he or she wants to tell her something. There will be time later to share her own working day, after she has first listened attentively to the child.

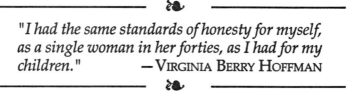

"I had the same standards of honesty for myself, as a single woman in her forties, as I had for my children." — VIRGINIA BERRY HOFFMAN

11. *A mom should never believe her actions at work or at home do not affect her children.* When frustrations and anger build up for Mom, those emotions are often "taken out" on the children. This may not be done in overt yelling and screaming; it may come forth in the disguised form of inattentiveness, impatience, or indifference. In the same manner that a parent who has been abused as a child may also abuse his or her own children, the mother who is being psychologically abused by a boss at work might inflict that same treatment on her children. Unhappiness breeds unhappiness, and if a mother finds herself in an unhappy working situation, either at home or away, she should take a close look at how she may be transferring her feelings to her children.

A mother's lack of honesty, fairness, and commitment at work also affects her children. If the mother brags to the children about what she is able to get by with at work, she is setting an example for her children which she may regret in later years. One mother let her children know that she always took longer lunch hours than she was entitled to because her boss was out of town most of the time. She also stocked her own desk at home with supplies from the office which she carried home at the end of the day. The same mother was appalled when she was called to school because her son had been caught stealing from another student's locker.

> *"Teaching children to be truthful is so important. My husband always said to our boys, 'You come home and tell us the truth, and no matter what happens, we will always back you up.'"*
> —MARY IDA PHAIR

Whether a mother works at home or in the marketplace, she needs to perform her tasks in the same honest, upfront way as she would want her children to perform theirs. Remember, moms teach more by their actions than by their words.

12. *A mother should always ask for God's guidance at home and at work.* She should ask for help from other people, as well, when she needs it. A mother should never feel all alone.

Philippians 4:6 states, "Do not worry about anything. But pray and ask God for everything you need. And when you pray, always give thanks." What a powerful Scripture for mothers.

When one mother of three teenagers was asked to comment on that verse she said, "Quite honestly, I have a very difficult time trying to apply it. I've always thought worrying just goes with the territory of being a mother. It will take a lot of faith for me to just pray and turn all my worrying over to God."

Most of us can probably relate to her honest answer. I would doubt that any mother has ever lived who hasn't worried about a child at one time or another. But what a comfort to know that we are invited to pray and ask God for everything we need. Those needs may be anything from how to better communicate with our children to how to make more money in order to send a son or daughter to college.

> *"If there is one thing that I could say to young mothers, it would be to not only look out for the physical and mental needs of their children, but to look out for the spiritual needs as well."*
> — BEVERLY GODDARD

A mom should also ask for help from other people when she needs it. One mother related the story of having a special Christian friend who was a great woman of prayer. When this mother was worried about a problem one of her children was having, she called this friend and ask her to pray about the problem, too. In telling the story, the mother said, "I've seen so many miracles happen in my children's lives, I know the prayers of my friend helped to bring some of those about."

13. *A mom should always remember that nothing can defeat her that she can praise God for.* She should praise God daily for her family, her home, and her work. When my children were small, my former pastor, Dr. William Goddard, preached one Sunday morning on the power of praise, and

I have never forgotten his message. He took his text from 1 Thessalonians 5:16–18, which states, "Always be happy. Never stop praying. Give thanks whatever happens. That is what God wants for you in Christ Jesus." Recently when I had an opportunity to visit with Dr. Goddard again, we discussed this passage, and I related to him how helpful it had been to me throughout the years. Dr. Goddard repeated the words from his earlier sermon, and this time I wrote them down: "Whatever you can be thankful for has lost its power to defeat you."

"To me, the key to motherhood is the wearing of your knees." —MARLENE HUFFMAN

Brenda, a young mother of a one-year-old little girl, tells the story of how she had hated to go back to work when her six-week maternity leave came to an end. Since her husband was only beginning his career, her salary was a necessity. For weeks, she cried each morning as she left her baby and went to work. She began to hate the job she had once enjoyed. Realizing she was going to make herself ill, Brenda started looking for ways to deal with her situation.

First, she made a list of all the positive things about her job, her family, and her life. After she compiled her list, she placed it in her purse. Each morning as she rode the subway to work she would get her list out, and naming them one by one, she would thank God for each item on the list. She related her story nearly a year later to a group of Christian working mothers, and told them how amazed she was at the difference that praise had made in her life. Instead of dwelling on how badly she felt about leaving her baby, she started thanking God that she had a baby to come home to. Instead of hating her job, she started thanking God that she was able to contribute to her family's financial needs. The very things which were once defeating her became gifts for which she could give God the praise.

11

Learning to Communicate

Eight emotion-packed words are, "I just can't seem to communicate with you." Most of us either have sent or received these words at one time or another, and we know the wide range of feelings they can produce: disappointment, anger, frustration, impatience, hurt, and inadequacy are some we might recall. If these emotions result from a lack of communication, then logically one would think we would all see the importance of learning to communicate. Maybe one of the reasons we don't is because we think *we* already know how — it's just *the other person* who doesn't. The other person probably feels the same way.

After working with parents and students for years, I finally came to the conclusion that every parent and every child should participate in a weekend seminar which focuses on developing communication skills. It should be an admission requirement, like the polio shots are. I feel this way because I have seen how crippling a lack of communicating can be — as crippling to the mental health as a germ is to the physical health, and sometimes as deadly.

The reason given most frequently by parents when asked why they are not enjoying their children is, "I don't understand them." When asked why this is so, the next answer is, "because I can't communicate with them."

Similarly, when mothers are having problems at work, a common complaint is, "I feel left out. I don't seem to be able to communicate with the people I work with all day." To help mothers at home and at work, this chapter will address ways to become a better communicator.

Forms of Communication

In the 1920s Dr. Paul Rankin identified and analyzed the frequency of use of the four major forms of communication: reading, writing, speaking, and listening. His research revealed that listening is clearly the most-utilized communication behavior. Other researchers have substantiated this finding. Dr. Ralph G. Nichols, known as "The Father of Listening," has revealed that listening has continued to be our first-learned, most-used, and least-taught communication activity.

Researchers have continued to give us interesting information about listening. Three facts to remember are:

1. Most people think four times faster than they listen, and they listen faster than they write.

2. It is estimated that the average adult gains 90 percent of his or her information just from listening.

3. Most listeners retain only 25 percent of what they hear.

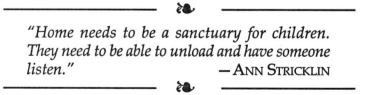

"Home needs to be a sanctuary for children. They need to be able to unload and have someone listen." — ANN STRICKLIN

Isn't it interesting to note that if we remember half of what we hear, we are twice as well off as the average listener! The next time your children say something like, "Oh, Mom, you never remember half of what I tell you," you can tell them how lucky they are to have a mother who is so far above average!

Active Listening

If we are truly interested in learning to better communicate with our children and our co-workers, we will need to work hard to develop a few skills of active listening. You can start by practicing the following suggestions:

1. *Be attentive when listening.* Focus your thoughts on the other person, and keep those thoughts from wandering. Do not daydream.

2. *Restate what you believe are the person's most important thoughts and feelings.*

3. *Listen for camouflaged feelings.* Many times, feelings are hiding behind words. Ask yourself what feelings you think you are hearing.

4. *Convey understanding of the other person.* Show it in your nonverbal behavior, such as nodding when appropriate, keeping good eye contact, leaning slightly forward.

5. *Put yourself in the other person's place.* Try to understand what the person is saying, how he or she feels, and the values involved in the situation.

6. *Avoid bringing up your own feelings and problems.* Young people are really "turned off" by having to listen to how it was in your day.

7. *Do not interrupt.* Allow the person time to express his or her full thoughts and feelings. Patience at this time is certainly a virtue.

8. *Do not offer advice or suggestions.* Often people only want to vent their frustrations. When they are ready for the problem to be solved, the solution should come from them.

9. *Have a desire to listen.* People will spot your fake interest. Develop the attitude that listening is fun and personally rewarding.

10. *Listen with respect.* This is especially true with a child. Adults tend to do most of the talking when conversing with young people, when they should be listening instead. Respectful listening shows dignity toward the children, allowing them to strengthen their own abilities to make decisions and solve their own problems.

Questioning

Mothers sometimes create barriers between themselves and their children by the type of questions they ask. "Why?" questions should be avoided, because they put the young person on the defensive. When a mother asks, "Why did you do that?" she may provoke anxiety, withdrawal, and half-truths from the child in his or her attempt to avoid criticism.

Other words to avoid at the beginning of sentences are "Did," "Have," and "Is." These words require a simple "yes" or "no" answer, and are not likely to stimulate conversation. Instead, try to begin a sentence with "How" and "What." A question like, "What do you think of the situation?" invites both a thinking and a feeling response. It builds self-esteem because it shows that the opinion of the child is considered important.

Along these same lines, mothers need to avoid giving their children pat answers such as, "Don't worry; everything will be fine," or "This happens to everyone at some time or another." While these may be truthful statements, they do little to make the child feel better. To the contrary, they may suggest to the child that what he or she is feeling is unimportant.

Communication Blockers

Without realizing it, a mother may react to her child's statement with a response that blocks communication. Some of these responses would involve threatening, blaming, preaching, analyzing, and avoiding. Let's look at an example of each of these barriers.

Threatening—"You'd better get your room cleaned now, or you will not go to the ball game." This type of response may invite the child to see if the mother really means what she says. Testing to see how far he or she can go may help open the door to rebellion.

Preaching—"You should have already taken that trash out of the kitchen." This statement communicates a lack of trust in the child's ability to develop his or her own sense of responsibility.

Blaming—"You are lazy, immature, and good for nothing." A child will not be inclined to have open communication with a mother who speaks to him or her in this manner. A fear of being criticized, as well as low self-esteem, will probably result.

Analyzing—"The reason you are acting like this is because you are not getting enough sleep." Communication is stopped as the child fears he is misunderstood.

Avoiding—"Let's not talk about that today. Let's just talk about happy things today." Again, this will make the child feel like his or her problems are unimportant, and it will not encourage him or her to be open and share feelings.

Skills to Practice

Listening is a skill which improves with practice. The main thing to remember is not to become discouraged when you find yourself doing some of these things which should be avoided. Just being aware of your mistakes will help you make them less frequently.

"My father had a motto, and when I was raising my children, it became my motto, too. It read: In the morning, think of your goal. In the daytime, do your best. In the evening, be thankful and keep love in your heart." —KATIE FUJITAKI

You may be thinking at this point, *I know what not to do; but what do I do?* When you are talking to your child, try to remember these four suggestions:

1. *Show respect.* Treat your child as you would like to be treated. By doing this, you will model the Golden Rule found in Matthew 7:12, "Do for other people the same things you want them to do for you."

Remember how it feels to be yelled at by your boss, and try not to do the same thing to your child. Let your children know that what they think is important to you, and you respect them and intend to treat them with dignity.

2. *Be aware of your tone of voice.* One young mother told a group of her peers how she had learned this important lesson. Just after the mother had completed a telephone call, her four-year-old took her hand and said, "Mommy, why don't you use that pretty-sounding voice when you talk to me?" Another mother shared that her teenager hid a tape recorder behind a box in the kitchen. He turned it on just before the mother arrived home from work, and later that night, he asked her to listen to it. She confessed that at first she was furious with her son, but when she listened to the recording, she was appalled at the way she sounded. She admitted that she had no idea she was using such a rough tone of voice. Later, she apologized to her son.

3. **Be brief.** One mother complained that her daughter did not listen to her. When asked why she thought this was true, she said, "I guess I talk too much, and it bores her." It is quite natural for parents to want to pass on wisdom they have learned over the years, but they often come across as lecturing. If you have a message to get across, leave space in your conversation for comments from your child.

4. **Be specific.** Strive to communicate in simple terms. When you are making requests of your child, make your message clear and to the point. Make sure your request cannot be misinterpreted.

Send Effective Messages

The previous statement leads us into another area of communication: sending effective messages. Personal relationships are often damaged or destroyed by the way messages are sent and received. These guidelines will help you to send effective messages:

1. *Use "I" statements to express feelings.* Mothers need to be reminded to "own" their feelings. An example of this would be saying, "I'm so angry when you don't complete your tasks," instead of, "You make me so angry when you don't complete your tasks." When we use the word "you" instead of "I," the listener will put up barriers because we have placed blamed on him or her.

2. *Be congruent with verbal and nonverbal messages.* In other words, make sure your body language matches your words. A congruent example would be when a person says he or she is fine and a smile is on the face. An incongruent example would be a frowning person who says he or she is fine. An incongruent message is often confusing because the receiver must decide whether to pay attention to the verbal or the nonverbal message.

"Mothers should talk to their children and listen to their needs. I always took my children to church, and I taught them right from wrong."
— DELLA BURNS

---

3. *Include "want" statements to express what you would like someone to change.* If the speaker does not convey explicit expectations about what is wanted, the receiver may believe he or she is powerless to resolve the situation. For example, if you want your son to get his hair cut, your request might be, "I'd like for you to get your hair cut Saturday morning, and I will be available to take you." If your request is more like, "I don't like your hair that long," then the problem may not be resolved on Saturday or any other day during the following week.

Decision Making

Along with the skills of listening and sending effective messages, a mother needs to know how to use decision-making skills, herself, and how to teach them to her child. Educators tell us that children and adolescents need to have the opportunity to practice making decisions in order to become self-directed, critical thinkers. When parents make all the decisions, children tend to see their lives as being controlled by others. This will hinder their attempts to make decisions later.

Let's take a situation that is probably familiar to most of us and carry it through a ten-step decision-making process. The example we will use is that you, a young mother, are trying to decide if you should go back to work. The ten steps are:

1. *Clarify your feelings.* Ask yourself how you really feel about going back to work, about providing added income for your family, and about childcare.

2. *Gather as much information about the situation as you can.* Is it necessary for you to go back to work now, or could you wait another six months? What job options do you have? How much money will each job provide you? Where will your child stay while you are away?

3. *Define the problem.* Is the problem that you want to go back to work and feel guilty about leaving the baby? Or is the problem that you don't want to go back to work, but the income is absolutely necessary? Or maybe you perceive a problem, but it really doesn't exist.

4. *Identify the decision.* If you have decided that a real problem does exist, write that problem on a piece of paper, along with the decision it calls for. If you have become aware that enough money is not in the budget for your family to live on, then the needed decision may not be whether you go back to work but rather where you work and when your starting date will be.

5. *Brainstorm alternatives.* You and your husband might borrow money from a relative or the bank. You might care for other children in your home so you could stay at home with your own. You might look for a business you could run from your home. Or you might choose to go back to the job you had before the baby was born.

6. *Evaluate the alternatives.* If you borrowed money so you could stay at home, how would you pay it back? If you kept other children in your home, would you be happy being so tied down every day? Would you enjoy having other children in your home? If you ran a business from your home, where would you get the money to invest in it? Would the new business make money immediately or would it take time? Is your previous job still available to you?

7. *Predict consequences.* If you go back to work and pay off your existing debts, you could quit in a year and stay home with your child. If you don't do something, the financial pressure on your husband may cause a strain in your marriage. If you take in other children, you could pay off your debts, and be at home.

8. *Clarify values.* You decide that you value the financial security of your family and the emotional health of your husband, so you will go back to work. You also value the time with your baby, so you will stay at home and care for other children. You decide that buying new clothes to wear to the office and having social contacts are not something you value very highly at this particular time in your life.

9. *Make an action plan.* You decide to put an ad in the paper and interview prospective mothers and their children. You decide to rearrange two rooms of your home to serve as a play room and a nap room for the children. You plan menus to have each week at lunch time. And you remember to make an application to have your home licensed.

10. *Follow up.* In a week's time you will see how many mothers you have interviewed and how many you still need to see. You will call the licensing bureau to see if all your paperwork is in order. And you will see if the expenses you are incurring are the same as the ones you projected.

This has just been a fictitious situation to show how each step is used; but I hope you see by using this example that any decision can be made by using the ten steps above. Going through these same steps with your son or daughter when he or she has a problem can be a real bonding experience.

Crisis Intervention

Most families will have some kind of a crisis at least once in their lives. Having a well-thought-through plan when that happens will make life easier for everyone.

When the 1989 earthquake hit San Francisco, a young mother was on her way home from work. Fortunately, she had already crossed the Bay Bridge into Oakland and was very near her older son's daycare center when the quake hit. After picking him up, she drove another few blocks to a private home to pick up her baby. The three of them then drove the short distance home, and anxiously waited for their husband and father to get home from San Francisco. This young mother's parents lived only forty miles away, but since the telephones were inoperable she could not contact them or her husband. It wasn't until after midnight that her weary husband was finally able to get through stalled traffic, take an alternate route, and get home. The young mother said that she had left work early that day to avoid the World Series traffic. When the ordeal was over, she realized if she had left at the usual time, she would not have been able to pick up her children until well into the night. With that frightening possibility in mind, the family later sat down and made out a plan of what each person would do in case another earthquake struck.

While earthquakes may not be an imminent danger to most people, other situations can be just as frightening and chaotic. A teenager who abuses drugs, an elderly parent who moved in with the family, a serious illness, or a divorce can also be a crisis for many people.

A crisis may be defined as a psychological state in which a person's normal coping or adaptive mechanisms no longer function. During a crisis, a person becomes very vulnerable because his or her basic human balance is disturbed. This imbalance may manifest itself in the physical body as well as the emotional being.

In the early 1940s, the crisis-intervention theory was developed by Erich Lindermann and Gerald Caplan. Crisis theory states that equilibrium achieved by a person in crisis is dependent upon the immediacy of treatment as well as the ability and effectiveness of the person who is intervening. Therefore, it emphasizes the importance of the support person dealing with the immediate situation without probing into the troubled person's chronic problems.

A mother should use the following steps when intervening in a crisis:

1. *Provide the most appropriate level of protection, security, and nurturing,* according to the person's obvious physical and mental needs. Activating help for survival and personal care is an important first step in a crisis.

2. *Evaluate the current situation* to identify the precipitating event. Discover what has happened in the person's life that has triggered the current stressful situation.

3. *Explore why the person cannot handle the current situation* as he or she has handled other problems in the past.

4. *Define the problem* in such a way that the person will understand and identify with it.

5. *Explore alternative ways of coping* with the problem and less threatening ways of viewing the situation.

6. *Lend appropriate support* to the person's efforts at managing or resolving the problem.

7. *Assist in the full recovery process* toward a restored balance and/or an improved level of functioning.

Crises may bring families closer together. By experiencing the depths of a tragic loss, the family members may realize how much they mean to each other. Growth often takes place when they learn to express their caring more openly to one another.

Resources in Your Community

Mothers need to become aware of resources in their own community and use them whenever appropriate. I have found it very helpful to have a card file on my desk filled with names, addresses, and telephone numbers of local agencies. When I become aware of a new service, I add a new card to the file. Over the years, my list of resources has become so extensive that I am now able to help friends locate hard-to-find services.

Some general categories you may want to include in your own file are library, police station, doctor, dentist, school, baby-sitting services, church, poison control center, drug information center, senior center, YMCA, YWCA, suicide prevention center, speech centers, adult education offices, animal shelters, allergy clinics, Big Brother and Big Sister organizations, the Braille Institute, child abuse information centers, counseling centers, the department of public social services, runaway shelters, hospitals, home nursing services, recreation department, and vocational training schools. You may not have need for too many of these services, but in case you ever do, you are prepared. You are also ready to assist someone else outside your family who may need a referral.

12

Having Backup Plans When Everything Is Going Wrong

No matter how organized, intelligent, talented, or capable a mother is, there will come a time in her life when things just seem to fall apart. This may happen to some mothers more frequently than it does to others and the degree of devastation varies; but every mother who is completely honest will admit that at some time in her career as a mother, she has just wanted to jump back in bed and pull the sheets over her head.

The first thing to remember in this situation is that you're not the first mother who has ever felt this way—and you surely won't be the last. In other words, you are not alone. And you are not a bad mother for having these feelings. Maybe you do need a day to pull the sheets over your head and rest! What's so bad about that? On the other hand, if a day's rest only compounds your problems by putting you farther behind the following day, maybe you need to take a look at what is really happening in your life. As we have discussed earlier, being a super-mom is usually not the answer, at least not for most people.

Valerie was a 1980s mother. She had been told by the media that women of her generation could have it all, and she believed the advertisements. She graduated from the right university, found the right job, and married the right man. She thought she was invincible. She dressed for success in clothes from top-name designers, and she wore them on a body that never carried a pound of extra weight. Her life was organized, with each event being planned well in advance. She wanted to have her first child during the fall, when her job was less demanding, and the baby was born on schedule.

All was well—until two years later, when her second child came along. This baby was sickly from the beginning, and the type of childcare provided for the older sibling was not satisfactory for this one. Three months later, her husband's company announced it was moving the main office to a southern state. Within less than a year, Valerie found herself in a new area of the country, away from friends and family, without the job which had brought her recognition and a substantial income, and at home all day with a three-year-old and a fussy baby.

"This is, indeed, the lowest point of my life," Valerie said to a women's support group which met at her church. "I've always been an achiever, and now it doesn't appear I'm going any place." Pausing for a moment, she gave a short, nervous laugh and then added lightly, "except to the grocery store or the cleaners."

In that same group sat Maggie, the mother of four children, all under the age of six. In contrast to Valerie, Maggie had never had a high-paying job. In fact, she had married right out of high school, and had never wanted any career except to be a good wife and mother. But things had not worked out exactly as she had planned, either.

When the real estate market collapsed in their city, her husband Jack, a construction worker, was laid off from his job. Maggie took a job making donuts at the all-night store nearby, but that meant Jack had to take care of the children while Maggie slept during the day. One afternoon when Maggie woke up, she found a note on the kitchen table from Jack. It said, "I'm sorry, Maggie. I never meant for our lives to turn out like this. I fed the kids lunch, put them down for their naps, and I'm leaving now. I just can't take being cooped up at home all day. I've got to try to find work in another state. I'll send money as soon as I get a job. Love, Jack." That note had been written six months earlier, and Maggie had not heard a word from Jack since. She and the children now receive a welfare check and food stamps, which cover only the essentials.

Barbara, a young mother of a two-year-old, is also in this support group; but her circumstances are different from either that of Maggie or Valerie. Barbara is doing exactly what she has wanted to do all her life. She is a schoolteacher who enjoys the stimulation of being in a learning environment. Her husband Norman is employed in another school as a dean of students. Together they share household duties and the care of their daughter, who stays in a daycare center during the day. Barbara tells her support group that she has an ideal arrangement, but she confesses that sometimes she feels very pressured. Because she does have so many good things going for her, she feels guilty if she ever complains about feeling frustrated or overworked.

Another woman in the support group is Alice, who stays home with a three-year-old son, but longs to go back to her job as a beautician. Both she and her husband feel her staying at home with their child is important, but she hates the boring routine of housework. How she misses the social chatter of a busy beauty salon! "Larry wants us to have another baby, but I don't think I could start all over and have to stay at home for the next six years. If we don't have a baby, I can be out of the house in another two years," Alice tells the group.

Four women sit together in a support group, each with her own needs — major needs, minor needs. But like the sand that gets in the traveler's shoes, even minor irritations can sometimes become major problems to the person who is experiencing them.

Let's look at some backup plans for overwhelmed mothers to use when everything seems to be going wrong:

1. *Make a priority list.* "Let go" of low-priority concerns. When Maggie discovered she was a single mother with four children to support, she knew she had to make major decisions about her life. Rather than "sit tight" until she heard from Jack, she mustered her strength and made a list of things she had to take care of. Food and shelter for her children took top priority. Since she knew she couldn't continue working at night, she immediately applied for welfare. She might be able to find a baby-sitter and look for daytime work, but she'd have to think about that later. Right now, her immediate concerns were feeding and clothing her children. She had never been on welfare before, and she began to worry about how it would look to her mother, father, brothers, and sisters. Would they see her as a failure? She allowed herself to dwell on self-pity for only a few minutes, and then she "let go" of that concern and started to apply her energy where it was really needed. By making her list, and worrying about only the high-priority items, Maggie soon felt confident that she could raise her four children alone if she had to.

2. *Use the resources available to you in the community.* Valerie knew that she could not stay at home all day and keep her sanity. But the doctor had told her the baby should not be placed in a daycare center until he was older and had time to outgrow some of the allergies which plagued him. Getting back into her professional world was very important to Valerie, but not as much as her son's health. Using the same organizational skills she had earlier mastered, she decided to research what options were available to her. A call to the large church she attended put her in contact with an associate pastor who told her about these services which the church offered:

- *Mothers Class.* A group of mothers meets two hours monthly. The first hour is an educational meeting focusing on issues that are relevant to young mothers. Sometimes specialists in various aspects of child behavior were invited to speak. The second hour was reserved for Bible study. Childcare was provided for a small fee. Valerie would attend this class; but she would leave the baby at home with a sitter because of his illness.

- *Women's Retreat.* From Friday night until Sunday, a group of women would occasionally stay at a church campsite in the nearby mountains and relax without husband or children. During this time, discussions and seminars would be held which would renew their spiritual lives.
- *Mommie and Me Class.* This class is available to the mother and her newborn to two-year-old child. Lasting from ten to twelve weeks, these sessions teach everything from how to bathe a baby to how to relate to a two-year-old.
- *Parent-Child Retreat.* Twenty-four hours are spent at a campsite by a mom or dad and one child. The emphasis here is on having the parent and child spend as much time together during those twenty-four hours as possible.

3. *Get away from the children for a weekend.* Barbara loved her child and she loved her work; but she needed time away from both. Rather than feel guilty about her thoughts of being overworked and frustrated, she decided to do something about it. Every six months she would get away for two days. One time during the year she would go on the women's retreat and the second time she would visit her sister in another city. Norman understood her need and willingly stayed home to baby-sit. Barbara reciprocated by insisting that Norman get away to his favorite fishing area at least twice a year.

4. *Limit your decisions until you can grasp the full situation.* Until she could find ways to be happy at home, Alice felt she wasn't ready to make a decision about having another baby and staying away from her job for six more years. In the meantime, she decided to see what type of business she could do from home in order to make her life there a little more exciting. Alice was a very creative person,

and after searching for ideas in magazines, she decided to do handwork and sell her items at craft fairs. She made everything from painted T-shirts to carved outdoor Christmas decorations. Her son was delighted with Mommy's new hobby and enjoyed making his own crafts from her scrap materials. Selling her handwork at the craft fairs gave Alice the social contacts she had been missing in the past. It wasn't long before she decided she'd like to have another baby.

5. *Take a day off.* Go shopping, get a new hairdo, clean out a closet, work in the garden, go parasailing, or engage in any other activity which refreshes you. Being at home with four children all day, Maggie knew that she needed a day off now and then. Every mother needs this, whether she has one child or ten. Sometimes it seems more difficult to obtain for the ones who need it the most, and this was certainly true in Maggie's case. Since she didn't have money to pay for a baby-sitter, she had to look for other alternatives. She found the solution to her problem by exchanging childcare with another mother in a similar situation. Not only did Maggie feel good about having a day to herself, which she usually used digging in her vegetable garden, but she also felt satisfaction in being able to allow another mother to have some time away, too.

> *"I would say to young mothers, 'Laugh a lot, even when you don't feel like laughing. Find some joy in everything.'"* — ANN BENGFORD

6. *Express your needs.* If there is no husband, find a friend and talk. Isn't it amazing how troubles seem to vanish when we're able to talk to someone about them? We are given instructions in Galatians 6:2 to "Help each other with your troubles. When you do this, you truly obey the law of Christ." Valerie was in a new city, away from family and friends; but she found a group of Christian women in the mother's support group. In these sessions she was able to

vent her frustrations and voice her fears and concerns, knowing this group would listen, be nonjudgmental, and keep everything she said confidential.

Barbara's husband was also her best friend, and they would talk for hours. He understood when Barbara expressed her concerns about their busy lifestyle and the pressures which came about because of it. He understood because he was actively involved in everything she was.

The mothers who do not have anyone to talk to are the ones who let pressure build up. If you do not have someone to share your thoughts and feelings with, find someone. A support group could be the listening ear you need.

"In raising children, you do the very best you can, you trust the Lord, and you never cease to pray for them, no matter what." — ANN STRICKLIN

---

7. *Do all you can to get things going in the right direction again.* After you have done your best, turn the problem over to God and leave your burden at His feet.

All four women we have read about in this chapter, Valerie, Barbara, Maggie, and Alice, had problems to overcome. Maggie's problems were monumental by most of our standards, but Barbara's seemed to be just everyday living problems—sand in the shoes. Valerie had to adjust to giving up an exciting career and making a move which involved a different lifestyle, and Alice had to decide what she really wanted out of life. All four women did all they could to make life better for themselves and for their families.

We, too, must do all we can to make life better for ourselves and our families, especially when things seem to be going wrong. There are times when it seems no matter what we do, life becomes more complicated. After asking for God's guidance to do everything we can, we must then turn loose of the problem and trust God to take care of it. In 2 Peter 5:7 we read, "Give all your worries to him, because he cares for you."

13

Enjoying Your Children — Enjoying Your Work

Some mothers seem determined to be miserable. They don't enjoy their work, their homes, or their families. In other words, they don't enjoy life. At least that's what they tell us by their constant complaints. Negative talk about one thing or another consumes their days. They feel overworked and unappreciated. There is never enough money in the bank to meet the bills, their kids are running away from home, their husbands don't listen or help, and their mothers-in-law are coming to visit. "Woe is me," is their theme song.

Before long, co-workers and neighbors go in the opposite direction when they see "Mrs. Unhappy" walking toward them. Her personality repels even the people who have tried to help her. How lonely her life must be.

Mrs. Unhappy may be the exaggerated version of many young mothers today. True, mothers often do have reasons to complain; but surely they can find a better way to tackle their problems.

Let's look at some situations mothers are talking about and see if there are ways to help them enjoy their children and enjoy their work.

1. *"Work is such a drag. I watch the hands on the clock move every hour and wish they'd turn twice as fast."*

If your work is making you miserable, evaluate your options. There is a difference in working at a job you don't particularly find interesting and working at a job that is unbearable.

Wanda knew she had to find a job quickly when her husband was laid off, so she took the first job she was offered — as a secretary for a crude, burlesqued, older man who was president of a manufacturing company. Nearly every day he would make some sexual remark to her, and before a month was up, he was making sexual advances. Wanda knew her husband would demand that she quit if he heard what was going on. She also knew there was a law against this type of behavior; but she didn't want to say anything to anyone because her job provided the only income her family had at the present time. Besides, she thought she could handle his remarks and advances.

Before long, though, Wanda, began to lose weight. Eating seemed to nauseate her. When she was home in the evening, her children got on her nerves. She became impatient with her husband's inability to find work. Her entire family suffered.

One day the secretary she had replaced stopped by to see friends. Wanda happened to be in the restroom at the same time as this former secretary, and they started a conversation. When the former employee found out that Wanda had been working for over six months for the president, she said, "I can't believe that you can take all the sexual harassment that man dishes out. I know I couldn't." Wanda's reply summed up her defeated attitude. "I don't have a choice. I have to work," she said.

What Wanda seemed to be missing was the fact that while she did have to work, she did not have to work at that particular job. Many times mothers will think they have no other options except to do what they are doing. Then, being miserable becomes a cloak they wear wrapped around themselves almost like a security blanket. Shedding that cloak is too big a risk for them to take, so they don't. Finally, misery becomes such a friendly companion that being happy is unfamiliar to them, and when they do have glimpse of it, they feel uncomfortable, undeserving.

There are options in every situation. True, sometimes the options are not obvious; but they can be found. Wanda had several options: (a) she could quit; (b) she could talk to her boss and let him know she did not approve of his actions; (c) She could report her boss to authorities, knowing he might fire her if he found out; (d) she could look for another job while she was still working; (e) she could ask her husband to take some temporary employment until he could get the job he was waiting for; (f) she could quit and go on welfare until she finds another job; or (g) she could tell her boss she wants to be moved to some other department in the company, even if it means getting less money.

Unfortunately, Wanda did none of the things listed above. She just stayed on and became more and more miserable. Finally, her marriage came apart, and her husband left town. Then she really felt trapped, because providing for her family was her responsibility totally, and she believed even more that she had to continue working at that job.

If you are in a job or a situation at home that is making you miserable, look at all your options. Remember that your mental health definitely affects your entire family. So it is not only unfair to yourself to remain status quo, but it is also unfair to your family.

2. *"My kids are driving me crazy. I sometimes wish I'd never had them."*

While this thought may have passed through a mother's mind at one time or another, for most it did not develop roots and remain. Unfortunately, for some mothers, it did. More than one time, I've heard a mother say, "John (or Mary) has caused me so many problems, I wish I'd never had him (or her) in the first place." Even worse, this statement was sometimes made in the presence of the child.

A mother who says these words did not intend for her life to be like this. When her child was small, she probably had visions of having a perfect parent-child relationship all through the child's teenage years. Somewhere along the way, though, the child began to behave differently than she had planned, and her own unexpected reactions surprised her. She had always believed that if she raised her child with her values and beliefs, he or she would turn out all right. But things had not seemed to work out that way. Now she was at wit's end and wished she'd never started on the journey.

> *"I think it is important to live close to the grandchildren. Kids need their grandparents, and parents need a break from the day-to-day stress."* — MARTHA SANFORD

A mother who is having serious problems may need to seek professional counseling for herself and her child. Without trying to determine who is right or wrong, who is to blame, or whose fault it is, probably all members of a family need to be involved in the counseling experience. Many situations have been resolved when a trained, objective, outside person is brought into the confidences of the family.

If a mother is home all day with small children, and feels like she is going crazy just because she is "on call" twenty-four hours a day, she may need a different type of solution. Sometimes a short vacation away from home will give her time to catch her breath and come back refreshed for another round. I highly recommend husbands and wives getting away together for a weekend. Some people resist this idea because of the cost, but it can be worth the expense if it helps resolve problems. It may be a matter of rearranging your priorities in order to do it.

One couple decided to forego their weekly night out and save the money for a short trip. Remember, I said forego the night out, I didn't say not spend an evening together.

Instead of a dinner out or a date at the movies, they planned special evenings at home after the kids were in bed. They would rent a movie or just curl up on the rug in front of the fireplace, eat a bowl of popcorn, and talk. They figured they saved at least twenty-five dollars each time they stayed in, which included the unused baby-sitting money. Within two months, they had accumulated enough for a weekend away.

If you feel like your children are about to "tip you over the wall," sit down and evaluate what you can do, or get them to do, differently. It may mean establishing a few rules, such as no one disturbs Mommy at her lunch time unless it is an emergency, or no calls to Mommy's office if you haven't tried to work the problem out first by yourself, or no friends visiting in the home after dinner.

Try to analyze what is getting on your nerves the most and work on that particular problem. If popcorn on the den floor makes you a little crazy, tell the children that food is off-limits in the den. If you feel guilty in doing this because other mothers let their kids eat anywhere they want to, then decide which you can cope with better, the mess or the guilt.

When you have resolved one problem, tackle another one. Don't try to resolve them all at one time. The main thing to remember is to keep trying. Children are not supposed to drive you nutty—well, at least not all of the time. Children are yours to enjoy. You just have to find the way to do that.

3. *"My life is so mediocre it's boring. I know I should feel grateful because I don't have any major problems, but how can I be thankful when I am bored to death?"*

This complaint is voiced not only by mothers and fathers but by their children as well. I was surprised to hear an eight-year-old say, "Life is so boring. All I ever do is go to school, come home, get my homework, eat dinner, and go to bed." What has happened to the joy of childhood?

Jesus said, ". . . But I came to give life—life in all its fullness" (John 10:10). Why is it that Christian people are not claiming this promise? If someone told us he or she had come to give us a million dollars, we would certainly look for ways of accepting that gift. Yet Jesus has come to give us something much more valuable than a million dollars. He came to give us life, and to give it to us more abundantly. We seem satisfied to just take life, but when it comes to the more-abundant part, we are not there to claim our portion. We miss the joy. What are some things we can do to get out of the rut of mediocrity and into the abundant life? How about trying some of the following things:

• *Have a time set aside each day for Bible study and prayer.* The common excuse for not doing this is, "I always intend to read my Bible and pray before I go to bed at night; but I'm so tired by the time I get all the chores done that I just jump into bed and go to sleep." I wonder what God thinks about being put off until the end of the day, and then having our fatigue get in the way of communicating with Him.

Why not set the alarm fifteen minutes earlier than normal and have those extra few minutes before the busy day begins to read the Bible and pray? Say a quick prayer when you are washing the dishes, making the bed, or stopping at a red light. Thank Him for simple pleasures and ask Him to continue to give you a more abundant life filled with joy and love.

• *Partake of some physical activity each day.* "I am really too tired to do that," groans the working mother of three. Maybe she wouldn't be so tired if she took a walk each day. We are told by doctors that exercise helps the different systems of the body function properly and stay in good working order. On the other hand, the lack of exercise can cause all kinds of symptoms, and one of them is tiredness.

If you are working away from home, you may want to take a short walk during your lunch hour. If you are an at-home mother, you may welcome the opportunity to get out of the house and walk, taking your children with you so they can run off some of their energy at the same time. If you live in an area where walking is not possible or where the weather does not permit it, you may want to get an exercise videotape and work out with the tape sometime during the day. Mothers who are at home report they are not alone in enjoying these tapes. Their preschool children see the exercises as something fun to try to imitate, and they join their mothers on the floor in front of the television set.

• *Do one activity a day that you particularly enjoy, maybe one you enjoyed before the children arrived.* You may have only fifteen minutes during the entire day to do this favorite thing, but that time will be well spent if the activity brings you joy.

One mother said that she takes a bubble bath and relaxes in the tub for twenty minutes each day. Before her children were born, she always enjoyed a tub bath, and she made up her mind after they arrived to never resort to a quick shower. "There are some pleasures in life that even children shouldn't take away," she says.

Another mother always carries her favorite, current novel in the car, and any time she has to wait for a child, she passes the time by reading. "I never realized how many minutes I waited in the car for school to turn out, for ballet lessons to be over, for Little League practice to end, or for piano lessons to be completed until I saw how much I could get read each week. I used to think I'd never have time to read another book until the children were eighteen; but now I am enjoying one of my favorite hobbies and using time that is not taken away from anything else."

• *Look for one other human being to help each day.* "What are you talking about? I don't even have time to help myself or my own family, much less someone else," the young mother complains. I didn't say it had to involve a lot of time or be anything complicated. A friendly hello and a smile may make all the difference to a grocery-store clerk who is having a hard day. A quick hug for a co-worker who is experiencing a minor crisis in her own life, or a cup of coffee and a listening ear for a neighbor may do wonders for the giver and the receiver. John 15:12 states, "This is my command: Love each other as I have loved you." Mothers who have an abundant life seem to always have time to reach beyond their own families to care for others in need.

"My husband and I want our boys to see our faith in action by our service and our love for others." —CAROLE STANNARD

• *Hug every member of your family, including your husband, at least once a day and say, "I love you."* How can life be mediocre when you have people to hug? God created Eve so that Adam could have a helpmate. Babies grow and thrive when they are handled and loved. Human beings need each other. As we reach out to other members of our families, we will find our own lives enriched, and we will understand better what Jesus means when He talks about giving us fullness of life.

4. One young mother said, *"I overheard my four-year-old daughter talking to her doll, and she was scolding her for not taking her nap. She used the same words and tone of voice she'd heard me use. In fact, she sounded so much like me it was scary."*

Model joy, happiness, and contentment to your children. Remember what *you* are may be what your children become. A group of mothers sat in a seminar discussing those two statements. Here are some of the thoughts they shared:

"I could hardly wait to reach eighteen so I could leave home," a mother of two said. "I just couldn't take my mother's nagging any longer. It seemed to me she was always on my case. I could never do anything right. I told myself when I had kids I'd never treat them like I was treated;

but the strange thing is, I do. Every day, I hear myself sounding more and more like my own mother."

"All I've ever wanted is just for my children to be happy," said the middle-aged mother of four. "But none of them really seems to be. They are all working and living productive lives, but none of them seems to have any joy. Of course, I was always too busy working as a single mother to really enjoy them, myself. It was always all I could do to just keep bread on the table. I guess there really wasn't much joy around our house. Maybe they would be happier now if they'd learned how to enjoy life when they were growing up."

"For as long as I can remember, all I have ever wanted was to just get married and have babies. Now I am married and I have a child and one on the way; but I also have something else. I have a full-time job." —DAWN BRAINARD

"I have a sister who is the happiest person I know," said the mother of two. "When we were growing up, we talked about our dreams and what we wanted to do someday. I always wanted to be an actress, marry a successful man, live in a fine home, and have two beautiful children. All my sister ever wanted was to get married, have a house full of kids, and stay at home with her family. I used to think she had no ambition. Ironically, we both got exactly what we said we wanted. I'm not a star, but I do get jobs as an actress. My husband is an attorney, we live in an expensive home, and we have two beautiful children. In contrast, my sister is married to a man who works at the post office; she has five children, they live in a small, three-bedroom home, and she stays at home and baby-sits other people's children as well as her own. Her house is clean, but always cluttered with projects. Yet that is the happiest home I've ever seen. She cooks simple, but wonderful meals, and there is always such lively conversation at the dinner table. In fact, my sister laughs a lot, and I think the entire family has picked up her sense of merriment and joy."

Think about the future in terms of twenty or twenty-five years from now. Imagine visiting the homes of your children, and observe what is happening in those homes. Are they filled with joy and contentment? Are your adult children modeling to their children the things that you modeled to them? If so, are you pleased with what you see? If the answer is no, remember it is still the present, not twenty or twenty-five years from now, and you still have time to change what you are modeling.

5. *"I wish we had more luxuries in life. As hard as my husband and I work, it seems we only make it from one payday to another. At this rate we will never be able to accumulate some of the finer things of life."*

Say your prayer of thanksgiving to God every morning and night. Thank Him for your health, for your ability to work, and for the endurance to be both a working woman and a parent.

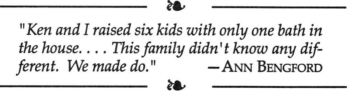

"Ken and I raised six kids with only one bath in the house. . . . This family didn't know any different. We made do." — ANN BENGFORD

Whether you work at home or in the marketplace, you are a working mother. Thank God for that privilege. In Ephesians 5:20, we read, "Always give thanks to God the Father for everything, in the name of our Lord Jesus Christ." Instead of thinking about the possessions you do not have, think about the truly important things in your home: your husband, children, faith in God, family devotion time, laughter, meals shared together, love for one another. When you weigh these things against material possessions, you will find that God has been very good to you. He has given you the greatest gifts of all.

14

Enjoying Your Adult Children

"When our children reach eighteen or graduate from high school, whichever comes first, we take them out to dinner and have an emancipation ceremony," said Gordon Bear, a licensed clinical social worker.

"What's an emancipation ceremony?" asked his friend Stan Morris.

"It's like a rite of passage," Gordon explained. "Each child enjoys dinner with one or both the parents, and when the meal is completed we spend another hour or so explaining what it means to be emancipated. During the evening, we also help them work out a plan for their future. After the discussion is over and we have prayed, the child is emancipated."

"Just what does it mean for the child to be emancipated?" Stan asked.

"It means the father and mother no longer view the child as a dependent minor. It also means that we no longer have a parental responsibility to the child, and they no longer have to be accountable to us as parents. They will be free to make their own decisions, and we will not interfere."

"Even if you don't agree with them?"

"We will give our children counsel, as we would any friend who asks for it; but that doesn't mean we will tell them what to do. Our children will know us as mother and father, but our interactions with them will be as adult friends."

"Do you think this type of thing really works?" Stan asked.

"I know it does," Gordon said. "We have emancipated three children, and they are all wonderful Christian young people who have a keen sense of love and service to others."

"Do you see them frequently?"

"We see the two boys every day because they live with us while they go to college," Gordon explained. "And we see our daughter on holidays when she comes home from college."

"The boys are still at home, even though they are emancipated?"

"Yes, but we do not parent them. Besides going to college, they work doing gardening and caring for the pool in exchange for their room and board. They are adults living at home; they are guests in our house. The relationship is great, and we enjoy all the children tremendously."

Another family has a different rite of passage. One of the sons explains the ritual at his home:

"As we were growing up my parents had always told us that once we graduated from college, they were "breaking our plate," and there would be no more "free lunch,"" said Kevin Brown.

"When my twin brother Kenneth and I graduated from college, Mother and Dad presented us with a gift. We each received a framed, broken plate, one we had eaten on while growing up. The three pieces of china were placed together in the shape of a plate, but the pieces were far enough apart that one could see they were broken. On the back of each frame was taped a substantial check to get us started in life and a message which said, 'It is with great joy and satisfaction that we present to you this symbol of love and affection. The world is now your oyster—open it and enjoy. We love you. Mom and Dad.' Thankfully, during a few financially difficult times since then, our parents have conveniently forgotten the plate is broken."

Both of these Christian families used symbols to tell the children they were now adults and they would be enjoyed in this new role.

Most of us do not use such graphic ways of letting our children know they have passed from childhood to adulthood; we just gradually "cut the apron strings" until one day we notice that our children are independent adults, living their own lives.

"Our children are living at home now, and the same people who criticized us for having my parents live with us are telling us now that the children shouldn't live at home; but that's all right. We are thoroughly enjoying them as adults, and our arrangement works out beautifully for all of us." —Armi Lizardi

---

However, a strange phenomenon has come about in the last two decades. Adult children who have left home are returning to the nest. According to the U.S. Census Bureau, twenty-two million young adults are now sharing the same household as their parents, which is a 50 percent increase since 1970. By the mid-1980s, over half of all young men age twenty to twenty-four were living at home.

Several factors seem to have contributed to the young people returning home:

1. Young people are waiting until they are older to get married, and therefore, they are waiting longer to establish their own households. In 1960, 72 percent of women between the ages of twenty and twenty-four were married. In 1984 only 43 percent of women in that age group were married. Among young adults age thirty to

thirty-five, the percentage of people who have never married has doubled since 1970.

2. The economy of the country has changed dramatically. The cost of living has increased 267 percent since 1970. College costs have soared, and many young people have needed to make sacrifices in order to help pay for college. Living at home has helped them to be able to repay college loans.

3. Entry-level salaries have not kept up with entry-level housing costs. Young people starting out on their own are finding they cannot make the budget stretch from one payday to the next. Living in the parents' home is the answer for many.

4. Young people have become accustomed to a certain lifestyle, and when they are living on their own they cannot keep their same standard of living. Back in the fifties, children worked hard to have a better life than their parents had. They looked forward to moving up. Now, young people would be happy to just remain at the same standard of living they had as they grew up. However, many of them know this will not be possible. Parents want their children to be financially secure, and in order to help them achieve this, they invite the children to live at home and save money.

Many parents bemoan the fact that their children have returned home, while many others look at it as a wonderful opportunity to enjoy their children as adults, without having all the responsibilities they had in the previous years. The parents who seem to enjoy their adult children living at home usually have made agreements with the children as to what is and is not expected of them. Some of the things parents mention which they think are important to resolve with their sons or daughters are:

1. *Will the adult child pay rent?* Families differ widely on this question. Some parents say they could never charge their own children for living in their home. Just the thought of it is repulsive to them. Other parents feel they are not being fair to the children if they don't charge them rent. These parents say the children will have an unrealistic view of life if they are not required to contribute.

Parents who charge for room and board usually request a very nominal amount. After all, the children usually are living at home in order to save money, and if the parents require the same amount the children would pay to live in an apartment, nothing would be gained. Most commonly, a fee of between one hundred and two hundred dollars is charged by the parents. Other parents collect rent, put it in a savings account, and give it to the child when he or she moves away from home. Many of these parents do not tell the children the money is being saved, and only later do the children find they have a wonderful surprise which will help get them started in the world.

2. *What household duties will be expected of the child?* Again, this varies with the individual family, but most frequently the adult child is expected to keep his or her own room neat, share the responsibility of common rooms, do laundry, and sometimes cook for himself or herself. Most adult children do not expect the mother to take care of their needs, but some may if the rules are not spelled out from the beginning. One mother who loves to cook invites her living-at-home son to eat all of his meals with the family because she enjoys having her food eaten. Another mother tells her child that he is invited to eat when she cooks, but she does not intend to cook every night just because he is home.

3. *Who pays the telephone bill?* Most families I have talked to think it is much easier for the adult children to get their own phones with private lines, and pay their own bills. "It was just too difficult to try to separate the long-distance phone calls and to let Matt know the amount he owed," said Peggy, the mother of an adult child. "But when Matt got his own tele-phone and had the bill sent to himself, the problem was solved. I no longer had to collect phone bills, which I hated to do."

4. *How often and when may friends be in the house?* The size of the house may make a difference when considering this question. Marsha lived in a large home, and when her son Tom invited his friends over there was always space for them to be in another room. Marsha never felt her

privacy was invaded by the friends. On the other hand, Ruth had only a small cottage, and when her daughter, Molly, invited friends over, Ruth felt displaced in her own home. Her bedroom was the only place she could retire to, and the only television set was in the living room. While most parents want their children to be able to invite friends to the home, they feel certain rules should be in place so the privilege will not be abused.

5. *What general rules must the adult children abide by?* Most parents do not set any limitation on the time the adult children must be in at night; but they do ask the children to tell them when they are going out. Basically, the parents ask for the same courtesy from their adult children that the parents show to each other. Notes are left on the refrigerator door to say where the other person is. Telephone calls and other messages are relayed promptly, and each one picks up after himself or herself. Anything that irritates either the parent or the child should be talked about and solutions should be sought before a real problem has time to develop.

James and Lisa Lizardi are two young people who live at home. James is twenty-three years old, a graduate of UCLA, and a member of his dad's successful advertising business. Lisa is twenty-one, attended a school of arts and design, and is also employed by her father. James lived away at school for four years, but returned home when he graduated. Lisa has always lived at home, but has talked about moving to her own apartment at various times. When talking to these young people, I asked them what they thought were the pluses and minuses of living at home. Here is their conversation as they discussed the subject:

JAMES: My biggest reason for living at home is financial. It's not that I can't afford to live in an apartment, because I really can. The big question is, Do I want to spend five hundred a month for just a place to sleep, or do I want to put that money in the bank and buy my own place later on?

LISA: And our parents make us feel real welcome. They never put any pressure on us to leave or stay. In fact, when I've talked about leaving, my dad has told me to do what I want, but to look carefully and see if it really makes sense for me to leave.

JAMES: We have great parents, and we all get along fantastically. If we didn't, living at home would be something altogether different. I know some of my friends are living at home, and they do not have the good situation I have. In fact, when they come over and my parents are so nice to them, they tell me they are jealous of my family life. I'm well aware that not all kids living at home have it as good as Lisa, Mindy, and I do. (Mindy is their nineteen-year-old sister who is also living at home while she goes to college.)

LISA: We have a lot of respect for our parents.

JAMES: That's another point. I have a lot of friends who live at home but who stay at their girlfriend's apartment nearly every night. I just won't do that. Even though my parents don't enforce rules which keep me from it, I know they wouldn't approve, and I wouldn't do something I know they wouldn't approve of.

LISA: And our parents don't give us pressure to live by their set of rules.

JAMES: That's just it. Because they haven't given me pressure, I don't feel like I need to rebel. I feel there is a mutual courtesy and respect in our family.

LISA: A lot of kids who live at home feel like their parents owe them something. Their attitude is almost like, You had me, now you support me. But I don't feel that way at all. My parents are doing me a big favor by allowing me to remain at home. Once I turned eighteen, they didn't owe me anything. They invite me to stay because they want to, not because it's their duty to provide for me.

JAMES: I know a lot of kids who totally abuse their home situation. They don't live in an apartment because they can't afford it; but they seem to resent the fact they can't have their own place.

LISA: Some kids don't even do their own laundry. They expect their moms to continue to do all the things they've always done for them.

JAMES: We are all very independent people in our family, and although we are together a lot at work and at home, we don't impose on each other—at least, we try hard not to.

LISA: There are times though, when I'd like a little more time to myself. Sometimes when I come home from work, and I'm really tired, I'd just like to go to my room and be alone. But there is usually someone knocking on my door or someone just wanting to talk.

JAMES: Of course, there are a few problems with any living situation. The hardest thing about living at home isn't the parents; it's the brothers and sisters.

LISA: That's right! It's things like my sister borrowing my clothes or my brother using my hairdryer. It isn't the big things, just little things that are annoying.

JAMES: Another thing that is annoying is having someone park their car behind me in the driveway. With all of us having cars and living at home, there are five cars which regularly pull in and out of our driveway. I know this may sound trivial, but when I'm in a hurry, getting blocked in isn't funny.

LISA: But our driveway isn't any different than our neighbors' down the street, and their children do have their separate homes.

JAMES: True, Lisa. I know who you are thinking about. The parents have five children, ranging in age from twenty to thirty, and they are always at their parents' home. I asked one of them, who happens to be a friend of mine, why there are always so many cars at the house, and he said all the kids enjoy being there.

LISA: I wonder what motivated them to move out, since they're at their parents' house most of the time anyway. They even spend the night there a lot of the time.

JAMES: That is certainly different from my girlfriend's situation. When she left to go to college, it was kind of like a final goodby. Two years later she transferred back to a university in her home town and asked her parents if she could move back into her old room, but they told her no. They insisted that she get an apartment, even though it was only a few blocks away. She really enjoys visiting my parents' home because there is an entirely different atmosphere of acceptance.

LISA: Maybe they were trying to teach her independence and to care for herself.

JAMES: Maybe so, but I think kids start feeling like they aren't wanted, and the relationship with the families becomes somewhat distant.

LISA: I think kids can learn to be independent living at home, particularly if they are responsible for their own finances and take care of their own personal needs.

JAMES: Some kids don't seem to want to be independent while they are living at home. I'm thinking of one friend who lives at home, and his mother does everything for him. She cooks all his meals, washes and irons his clothes, changes the sheets on his bed, cleans his room. He couldn't have it better as far as having everything done for him, but he isn't happy. He wants to move out. Maybe that's the secret. If a person isn't independent while living at home, no matter how nice it is to have everything done for him, he won't be happy.

LISA: An area that we haven't talked about is whether a person should pay rent to the parents.

JAMES: I try to pay for some things, like groceries, but I don't pay rent. When I've asked my parents about it, they've always said no. Even though I've offered a lot of times, they've never wanted to do it. But I think I'd really like to. It would give me even more sense of responsibility and independence.

LISA: I feel the same way about it. I buy things, too, like groceries, washing machine soap, things like that, but I'd really like to pay rent.

JAMES: It may be hard to convince our parents to take it.

LISA: One thing I'd like to talk about is how special living together is for all of us now. My dad always worked long hours when we were small, and my mother did most of the child rearing. Now we are working with Dad, and we get to spend time with him. He loves it, and so do we. If we didn't live at home, my mom would be in a five-bedroom house all alone most of the time, because Dad still works long hours. I'm sure she'd be lonely. With us home, there is activity in the house. It really works out well for all of us.

Children are to be enjoyed at every age from infancy to adulthood. The problems are different with each age, and just because the children are grown doesn't mean there still won't be strains on the parent-child relationship every now and then. But as the problems are worked out, the way is paved to continue enjoying the children.

"I don't know which stage of parenting is the most enjoyable; each one just seems to get better and better." —JEAN ROCKETT

Rose, the mother of four grown children, put it this way: "I wouldn't think of not enjoying my grown children. After all, I've earned the right. I've stayed up nights with them when they were sick. I've washed their clothes, ironed, cooked, listened to their problems, and wiped away their tears. They've turned out to be real nice adults, and I get to reap the rewards of all my labors. I enjoy them more now than ever before."

15

Hearing from the Mothers

Mothers have always talked to each other. They have shared their concern, joy, pain, excitement, love, and knowledge with their sisters, cousins, and friends. Mothers have also passed on child-rearing tips to their own adult daughters, and their wisdom has flowed from one generation to another.

As I have talked with mothers across the nation, I have realized what vast reservoirs of expertise these women possess. While they all hold dear a common bond of Christian faith and principles, each mother has her own unique ways of dealing with her children, husband, home, and work situation.

I have received permission from these women to include some of their child-rearing tips, thoughts, and suggestions in this chapter. I purposefully have included words from a wide variety of mothers: new mothers; mothers of two, three, four, or more children; mothers who combine child rearing with a career, and others who do not; young mothers; middle-age mothers with grown children; older mothers; single mothers; and married mothers.

This chapter is meant to serve as a smorgasbord of ideas from which you may choose and apply to help in your own situation. It is really more than that, though. It is a place where you can hear from real mothers, using their own names, who openly and honestly share their philosophies in hopes that in some way they may be helpful to you.

Let's read what these mothers have to say.

Joyce Penner
Therapist, author, speaker
Wife; mother of three children: Julene, twenty-two, a senior at Harvard University; Greg, twenty, a sophomore at Georgetown University; and Kristine, thirteen, an eighth grader

What a joy it is to be a mom! I believe children are not ours to possess. They are a gift to nourish, teach, guide, love, take care of, and move from being dependent to independent.

The important thing is to really enjoy your children, to delight in them. To me, how you feel about them makes the difference in how the children feel about themselves. And how they feel about themselves will affect how able they are to develop their natural abilities and relationships with others. Obviously, all are born with different abilities and dispositions; but I think there are children of equal intelligence, of equal giftedness, of equal tenderness who get lost along the way. They don't feel good about themselves because the parents don't delight in them.

When our first two were little, I had to work because Cliff was in graduate school, and it was interesting for me at that time to watch my friends who were not working. I could hardly wait to get home from work to be with my children; I was so excited just to see them. In contrast, I saw the other mommies being so frustrated after being with their children all day that it relieved some of my guilt about having to work. What I did was to tune into the idea that when I was with my children I would give them quality time, even if that meant hiring household help so I could have more time with them. Now many young moms will say, "But we can't afford household help." Let me be quick to say we started to hire help when we were in graduate school. We lived on the bare essentials, no TV or new household possessions. We had an old, secondhand car. But our family was our priority.

Take special time with each child; take special time with your family and with your husband. Build positive memories and experiences.

One thing we did, which I'd like to teach young mothers to do now, was to develop family traditions. As the children went through adolescence, the traditions we had developed kept our family connected. For example, when they were little, Saturday was family day. As they got older, we always had family time on Sunday nights from five until seven. Family time could vary from going out to dinner, to having family devotions, to just talking about some issues or having calendar-planning time. The main thing was that we were always there together, no matter what was happening. Other traditions included tucking the children into bed, having breakfast together—anything that connected us.

Be there for your children. Walk alongside of them. Give of yourself to them. When kids are first confronted with a new task which feels overwhelming, it is very important for the parents to be there to support them and to guide them through it step by step. It may be a new homework assignment, a music practice, or a new skill to develop in sports. Some parents may think this is helping the child too much;

but if you help in the first round, they have the confidence and model to become self-sufficient and do it alone.

Our children have succeeded academically. That is an extra blessing, not a necessity to happiness or fulfillment. We have never put pressure on our kids for grades; they have never gotten rewarded for grades except for us to be proud of them. Grades have never been the issue. The main thing has just been to encourage them with their homework, to be excited about what they are learning, and to be thrilled with the process rather than with the resulting grades. I believe in high expectations with constant support and encouragement, rather than pushing, demanding, or punishing.

The family unit is important to me. I never allowed my children to fight—at least, not for long. Our first two children are very close in age, and I'm sometimes asked what I did about sibling rivalry and jealousy. They had plenty of both. If they started fighting they went into their own rooms. The timer would go on, and they could come out in five minutes and try again. I think children can really destroy each other's self-esteem. Human nature is such that siblings can say awful things to each other if the parents allow them to do that. I always told them that I was there to have a good time with them, and I didn't want any fighting. Sometimes parents get so wrapped up in their own roles of doing everything right that they don't see what the siblings are doing to each other.

Being a mom is *hard* work! It is the hardest work you'll ever do in life, but it is also the most fulfilling.

Most people feel that you teach children responsibility by giving them chores. I don't think that is wrong, but we just did it a little differently. Because we had live-in help, we didn't have chores to do. So we tended to teach the kids that their responsibility was their schoolwork and their activities. In the same way that I'm responsible for my job, they were responsible for doing their tasks well. We taught them to do well at whatever their life function was at the time, whether that was school, or practicing music, or participating in sports. I am grateful they learned responsibility in this way.

Give to your kids—give of yourself, your time, your ears, your heart.

Carole Stannard
Former elementary-school teacher
Full-time wife and mother of two children: Tyler, four, and
  Lincoln, two

Bob and I feel that it is important that I am in the home full time. Because we are Christians, we feel like the spiritual input is very important to give to our boys, especially in our society today. My being home will allow more time for that to happen, as well as give us more time to teach values.

Passing on our love for Christ to our children is what Bob and I want to do. We are both from non-Christian backgrounds, and we did not become Christians, ourselves, until I was in high school and Bob was in college. When we first got married, we wanted to be missionaries overseas, but now we serve in an urban ministry. I attend Bible Study Fellowship with many women from urban ministries, and Tyler is in one of the classes they have for the children. We want our boys to see our faith in action by our service and our love for others.

Bob is a family-practice physician who works for an urban ministry in Chicago's West Side. This group serves in an all-Black neighborhood, and they are there to provide quality medical and counseling services to people who otherwise might not be able to afford it. He does this on a full-time basis, working most evenings until after the children are in bed. At first, it was difficult for me to be alone in the evenings without Bob's help, particularly when the children and I were tired at the end of the day. However, it became easier with my parents stopping by some evenings; other evenings they take the children to church activities. Grandparents have been very helpful and very supportive to the children and to me. I really appreciate living close to them. It has been a privilege for our children to get to know their grandparents.

We use music to teach our sons. Bob and I were brought up having musical backgrounds, and we find that music provides a great way to have fun with the children, as well as to teach them biblical principles through song.

Bob and I have found it to be very helpful if we sit down together at the beginning of the week and review our calendars. By doing this, our expectations of each other are more realistic.

At this time, I am planning on home-schooling our children. Before our children go into a public-school situation, we feel they first need to have a Christian foundation so they can be prepared for the things they are going to see in the world. We plan to move into the neighborhood where our ministry is, so this has bearing on the preparation our children will need. We'd like to have them home for schooling until they are at a point when they have either made a profession of faith or we feel they have enough of a spiritual background in order to face whatever may be put before them. When I was a public-school teacher, I saw how quickly children had to grow up in our society, and I don't want Tyler and Lincoln to be rushed through childhood. That is where we are right now; but I can't say where we may be a year from now with our decision about homeschooling.

Things get a little stressful with two active boys in the house, so I do things to break the pattern. I may ask them to join me at the kitchen table for activities such as doing crafts, painting, or baking, or we may go for a walk. It is very important at times for me to use these kinds of activities to redirect the energy of my boys.

Dolva Watson
Public high-school nurse
Single mother of three children: Rick, twenty-one; Dan, eighteen; and Rebecca, sixteen

After my divorce, I knew I had to go back to school so that I would be able to provide adequately for the children. At that time they were young, about seven, four, and two; but when I started taking chemistry and anatomy courses in preparation for becoming a nurse, I included the children in my studying. I talked to them using terms from the courses I was studying. It helped me to remember the terms, and the children thought it was great fun to say, "May I have a glass of H_2O?" instead of saying, "May I have a glass of water?" In learning the parts of the body for the anatomy class, I'd point to the various parts and we'd all say them together. I also taped all the class lectures I attended, and I'd play them while the kids and I were driving in the car together. The kids knew most of the bones in the body before I finished that course. Studying in this way allowed me to spend time with the children and learn my class material, too.

My self-esteem was very low after my husband left, and I really wondered if I would be able to get a college degree. But after I realized I could make A's and B's and have a good time with the kids while I was studying, my confidence grew. After I reached my first goal of getting my R.N., I went on to get my bachelor's, master's, and doctorate degrees.

I took my kids with me everywhere. When I enrolled in Valley College, they went with me. They were in the first group of children to attend the college's day center.

Every weekend, the children and I would do something together, something that was free. We'd comb the calendar section of the newspaper and see what was happening. The children really got quite an education during those early years, because it was usually a museum or a concert that would be free of charge. Sometimes we would go to a park and have a picnic, or go to the beach on Saturday, but we always went to church on Sunday mornings together.

We never had any money for a fancy vacation, but every year we took a trip. I had a big tent, and we'd go somewhere and camp out. It didn't matter where we'd go, just so long as we were all together and having fun. We'd take our own food from home, usually canned goods, and it wouldn't cost us any more than if we'd eaten at home. We never ate out because it was too expensive, but we were always able to do things. One year we went to Yosemite National Park.

The children and I always went to all the graduations in the family. No matter if it was a graduation from kindergarten or a college ceremony, we were all there supporting one another. It was good for the kids to see that I completed my work, and I graduated, too.

When the children were young, I was with them twenty-four hours a day, 365 days a year, because I didn't have any other family who could care for them. But when they got older, we were able to have some time apart. The children used to sell candy or peanuts and earn money for camp, and when the youngest one got old enough to go, they would all go to camp at the same time. It was at that time that I had my first week alone without them.

Our Christmas tree never had any store-bought ornaments on it. Each year we'd make new ones to add to the ones of the previous years, and when the children became older they could see their lives on that Christmas tree. I used to fill the children's stockings every Christmas Eve; now the children fill mine. It's a nice switch.

A single mother does what she has to do. It's not always what she wants, and she may wish that it didn't have to be that way; but in order to reach a goal so she can make a better life for her children, she may have to accept help from someone else. In my case, I had to go on welfare one time when the children were small. It was before I got my R.N. and I couldn't make enough money to support the children and continue to go to school. I didn't like to feel that I needed help, but the truth was I really did. In retrospect, I know that it was the only thing to do. I couldn't have continued to go to school and better the lives of my children if I hadn't accepted welfare.

Being a single parent has been difficult at times, but the children and I have always tried to make the best of things, and we've had a lot of fun along the way.

Lynn Walter
Engineer
Wife; mother of two children: Bryan, four, and Gary, two

I worked for six years as an engineer before I had children; I had waited long enough to where I was really enjoying my work, and I was well established in my career. I enjoyed what I did, I enjoyed the people I worked with, and, of course I enjoyed the money. So when Bryan was four months old, I went back to work. I took three months off when Gary was born.

Wayne is also an engineer and we work for the same company; but we don't ride to work together. We stagger our hours of going to and coming from work, so that one parent may be with the children an hour later in the morning and the other parent is with them an hour earlier in the afternoon. We share equally in parenting the boys.

We have used a variety of methods of childcare. My mother kept each boy during work hours for a few months when they were under a year old. We now have them at two separate places. Bryan is at a preschool, and Gary is at a licensed family home. We are fortunate that we are able to afford quality daycare for the children.

Once a week, I go to the grocery store around midnight because the boys are in bed and everything is quiet. I try to buy things that I can prepare quickly but which are nutritious for us, like steamed vegetables. When I cook, I allow the boys to climb up in chairs and help me prepare the food. It is an activity that we all enjoy doing together.

During the Thanksgiving and Christmas holidays, Wayne and I like to have our parents come to visit us. We like to be in our home and start our own traditions for the children.

My standards for housekeeping are not the same as my mother's, but when I work full time I want to spend time with the children while I am home. I enjoy playing with them. I go in their rooms, take their toys out of the closet, and we sit down and play. We are real playmates.

Virginia Berry
Counseling administrator
Wife; mother of five children: Phillip, twenty-six; Amy, twenty-five; David, twenty-four; Sarahbeth, twenty-three; and Molli, eighteen; stepmother to three: Kimberly, thirty; Tracy, twenty-eight; and Clell, twenty-three

I didn't work until my last child was three years old. I was home with my children when they were little, and that was really important to me. I am now going to be a grandmother, and I say to my girls, "Try to be at home with your children for the first five years." You never know what is going to happen in your life. I was divorced and a single parent for a while, and I never intended for that to happen. I look back, and I see how successful my children are with life now, and I think they are that way because of those first five years we spent together.

I was in a Bible study when my children were small, and the support I had from those women made all the difference in my life—and in my children's lives. It gave us a firm foundation spiritually as to what was important, so there was no question as the children grew up as to what the standards were. I think that made a tremendous difference in each one of their lives.

I had always wanted a big family, and my children have been the joy of my life. We didn't have any more holidays than anyone else did, but everything that happened became a celebration. On St. Patrick's day I would dye all of their food green. They would go to school, bite into their apple, and find a streak of green in it. I would pack love notes in their school lunches, and I'd hide little treasures underneath their pillows. The children knew they were special.

We touched a lot in our family; I hugged the children frequently. From my perspective as a counselor, I chose the role of the nurturing parent. I wanted my children to turn on to life. I tried to watch for things I'd see them doing right, and I would reward them. With punishment, I chose to spank because it was quick, it was over with, and it was a "done deal."

I didn't try to have perfection in the home. It wasn't *House and Garden* perfect, but it was a place that was picked up, and the children knew they could bring their friends in.

My mother loved to bake for her family, and I enjoyed baking cookies. When I first started to work, I remember rushing home, pulling out a plate of cookies, and sitting quickly on the sofa, so I'd be there when the children got home from school.

Parents have choices. We may choose joy; we may choose to love. We need to pause before we make choices, and make sure we are choosing the right ones.

After my divorce, I knew I had to financially support the children. I had to look where the money was and gear my career in that direction, because I had to make a financial impact. And I think God blessed my efforts. I was working full time, going to school full time, and I didn't have any household help. I had to organize and marshall the resources I had, and those resources were the children. At the time I felt a little guilty about it, because I expected a lot from them; but they monitored each other and they had high standards for keeping the house neat, probably higher standards than I would have had.

I was always on the couch when my children came home at night, and they knew I'd always be on that couch. Sometimes mothers can't go out as much as they'd like to, but parenting only lasts for a given number of years. However, those years may make the difference in what kind of lives our children will have.

When I got my divorce, there was a lot of anger, a lot of resentment, and a lot of hurt. The only thing that got us through was the fact that God loved us so much, and we chose honesty. I decided if I was going to be single, at least I was going to be honest with my children. There weren't going to be hidden agendas or misconceptions, so my children knew what was going on in my life. Another reason for sharing was that I didn't want the children to think my moods were a result of their behavior.

I had the same standards of honesty for myself, as a single woman in her forties, as I had for my children.

I am making soft-sculptured dolls to put away for my grandchildren-to-be. I want to make at least eight so there can be one in each family. I'm learning to crochet and have made two afghans, one for my son's wedding and one for my new grandson. When my grandchildren reach the age of three, I want to take each one to Montana with me for a month, without his or her parents. I want to get to know them as people, and I want to teach them how to sew, weave, plant a garden, make jam, build things, go fishing. I want to teach them all the things I like to do.

I gave each daughter a hope chest on her sixteenth birthday, because I knew one day she would be leaving our home, and I wanted her to have some treasures to take with her when she left.

Janice Gutierrez
Former advertising account representative
Full-time wife and mother of one child: Melissa, ten months
(Lynn Walter's sister)

I worked for seven years after graduating from college, but I did not go back to work after Melissa was born. I had decided before I got pregnant that I wanted to stay home when children arrived; I wanted to be involved in their development.

Dan and I made a lot of decisions before Melissa was born which have enabled me to stay at home with her. When we bought our house, we chose one that we could afford to pay for with one salary. We aren't living in our dream house or our dream neighborhood, like a lot of our friends are. We've made a lot of material sacrifices, but we both know that's what we want to do.

Staying at home is not a popular decision. There is a lot of pressure to continue to work. Most of my friends who have babies work all day, so I am kind of alone in staying home. I never find being at home boring, though; I can always find things to do that interest me.

I made a decision to stop working, not to be a maid, but to be a mom. Motherhood should not be equated with being a housekeeper. I stay home to be with my child, not to put her in a playpen while I do all the housework. Dan and I share in the housework in the same way we would if I had a job working outside the home. I'd hate to work now and regret later that I had missed all the years of Melissa's childhood. These are years that can't be relived later.

Melissa and I kind of plan our day by ear. It is very nice to have that flexibility. We may play inside, or we may go outside for a walk, or we may go visit Grandmother.

If I wasn't a Christian, I'd probably be working now, because the material things would mean a lot more to me than they do. Right now, I just feel very blessed. I feel God's presence and His pleasure in the love I have for Him, and in the love I have for Melissa.

Marlene Huffman
University school of nursing lecturer
Wife and mother of three children: Michael, twenty-seven; Lori, twenty-five; David, eighteen

John and I had been married five years when we adopted Michael. We had prayed so hard for a child, and Michael was an answer to our prayer. We continued to pray, and two years later we were able to adopt Lori. We had two beautiful children for whom we were very thankful; but I still had a longing within me to become pregnant someday. I remember lying in bed one night presenting my "case" before God, perhaps even arguing with Him. My thoughts in argument were of a young couple who had arranged to have an abortion. Following the abortion, they each had married someone else and proceeded to raise their families. I remember saying to God, "Lord, this just doesn't seem fair." There was a real struggle within me until I finally surrendered to Him and said, "Lord, I don't understand, but that's okay. You are in control, and Lord, I love You regardless of the circumstances." Two months later, I was pregnant with David. I had been married for fifteen years when David was born.

We feel strongly that the Lord only loans us our children, whether they are born to us or adopted by us. What special gifts they are, and as parents we are responsible to Him. One day Lori and I were talking, and she said, "I thank God every day that my birth mother did not have an abortion."

In every family, given enough time, there will be difficulties. I feel our relationship with our children would not be so special if we had not gone through certain difficult times. We need those experiences to build more meaningful and beautiful relationships.

One of the hardest things to do as a Christian mother is to put your faith and trust into action. It's so easy to say, "Yes, Lord, I trust You." But when difficult times come, we have a tendency to take back that trust and worry our way through the problem.

The Lord continues to show me how important it is to give our children up to Him and allow Him to work in their lives. The issue isn't, "Are we doing everything right?" but rather, "Are we willing to continue holding them up in prayer and trusting Him with our most precious gifts?" He works out everything that is committed to Him, in His own time. This may not be according to our schedules, and it doesn't mean we don't experience some pain in the process.

I found that it was very important when we were going through difficult times with the children to have a solid, mutually supportive relationship with my husband. We have a strong marriage, and we support each other and agree on the decisions we make concerning the children.

As mothers, we need to practice defensive praying. We shouldn't wait until something happens before we pray about it; we need to pray that it won't happen in the first place. To me, the key to motherhood is the wearing of your knees.

I've encouraged my children from the time they were young to pray for that special person the Lord would have for them as their life's partner. Marriage is a lifelong commitment, and I'm certain they don't want to end up with a "continual dripping on a rainy day" (Prov. 27:15). We talk to kids about defensive driving, and we need to talk to them about defensive living.

As a Christian mother, I feel it's not a matter of working or not working. It's a matter of establishing proper priorities. My first priority must be God; the second is my husband; the third is my children; and work comes after that.

We need to tell our children to expect great things from God. He promises the abundant life and how true that is when we wait upon Him.

Marcie Perry
Owner and manager of a monogram store; former beautician
Wife; mother of two children: Joey, eight, and Brian, six

I worked as a beautician until my children were born. Then, when the youngest was four, I went into my own business. I had always been creative with sewing and crafts, and monogramming was something I knew I could do. Now I have several employees. I could expand to other stores if I wanted to, but I don't want to do anything to take me away from my children more than I am now. Now I only work five days a week from nine until five.

When I was at home with the boys, I felt very sheltered. I didn't have a lot of outside influences, but since I've been in my store, I've learned a whole lot about business and about the world. It is very different when you're at home. I've learned so much in the past two years. I don't think I could have learned as much in four years of college. But it took me at least a year to get past the guilt I felt when I first went to work and left my boys. My husband works for an oil company, and I knew I didn't have to work; but I thought it was important for me to have money I'd earned.

My husband is excellent with the boys. He really helps me a lot, and when he is with them, I don't have to worry. But my kids need me, too, and I need to be with them.

Fortunately, baby-sitters have always really worked out for me. After Brian started to kindergarten, things really got a lot easier. My husband goes to work very early in the morning, and he gets out early enough in the afternoon to pick up the boys from school.

I make a menu out for two weeks in advance, and when I go to the grocery store I know exactly what I'm going to buy for each day's meals. It is important to keep the menu posted, because it's easy to forget what you bought certain foods for, particularly when you buy that far in advance. I've found that planning meals ahead of time saves my energy in many ways. I don't have to keep running to the store, and I don't have to try to think each day what to cook for dinner. On Wednesday nights when we go to church, my husband will make something simple for us, like hamburgers. Mothers have to be organized if they are going to work. Some days I get up at five-thirty in the morning so I can get food ready for our evening meal.

At our house, Saturdays are totally for the family, and those are good times for me. It kind of fills the void during the week when I'm so busy.

I think working takes a lot out of a woman, and it adds stress to the relationship with her husband because she is so tired all the time. My attitude about some things now is different than it was when I wasn't working, because then I wasn't so tired. When you work, you are so stressed out, so tired, and to me, it seems a woman's work never stops. A man can work his eight hours, go home, and clock out with TV or fishing; but a woman can never do that. A working woman changes hats so many different times, and her work is never ending.

A woman's working definitely adds stress to the marriage; but there are some good things that come from it, too. Men learn to take more responsibility when the wife is not around all the time, and that's good. Women can also be more independent, because they have an income coming in.

If I had a daughter, I'd definitely tell her to go to school and learn a skill, or prepare for a career, something she could fall back on if she needed to. Because whether it be from divorce, or death, or whatever, her whole life could be changed in a split second. I see so many divorced women who don't have any education or any skills, and it's so hard on their kids. I haven't ever been much for women's lib, but I definitely think a woman needs to have something she can use to make a living.

When children see their mom confident and happy, I think to a certain extent it builds confidence in them. My kids are proud of me in their own way, and they know I'm able to do things for them because I work.

A working woman has to keep her priorities straight. If she ever loses sight of her family, a woman has lost it. I don't care how big her business is or how small, if she ever sells out to something besides her family, she's messed up big time. There is really a fine line there sometimes, because working a few more hours may not seem that important.

I just kind of take my life one day at a time now. If the Lord sees fit to move me into something else, I will be willing. If He wants me to continue at my present business, I think He will keep me there. I had to give it to Him from the very beginning, anyhow. I want to do what the Lord wants me to do, and then I know everything else is going to fall into place.

Jean Rockett
Real estate agent
Wife; mother of four adult children: Renita, Bob, Dale, and Nicki
Grandmother of eleven children, ranging in ages from five to twenty-one

I was fifteen years old and Bud was nineteen when we got married, and I was a mother at sixteen. When the first baby was three months old, I took a job as a bookkeeper, and Bud and I rotated keeping her. We worked at different times of the day, and there was only a three-hour lapse where we had to have a baby-sitter.

Then World War II came along, and Bud went into the service. I stayed home with the children from that time until the last one went to school, and then I went back to work as a bookkeeper. In many aspects, our family wasn't much different then than families are today: Mom worked and Dad helped with the children and the house. From the very beginning, the entire family pitched in and helped with the chores. We made a chart every week with the kids' names on it, and they got stars when they completed their chores. It was like a game to see who could get the most stars.

When I started to work, I learned to make every minute count and to have a routine. One thing we were really firm about was that the children would not throw their clothes around. The clothes always had to be picked up and put away. Bud always helped me around the house, and we'd do the grocery shopping together. Grocery stores were not open to midnight then like they are now, so we'd have to schedule that trip in the daytime.

Our television was always turned off before dinner, and left off until everyone's homework was completed. If there was some program the children wanted to watch, and one child was lagging behind with his lessons, the other children would help until the assignment was completed. The children just all pulled together.

For the past twenty-one years, I've worked in real estate, and I really enjoy what I do. But I've always enjoyed my work. Working all during the time the children were growing up never really seemed to be a problem for me. Of course, women working then was not as popular as it is now, but we always did what we had to do, and things seemed to work out. Bud and I always shared in everything, and it didn't matter whether that was parenting, cooking, washing, or cleaning. He was a modern man before his time.

Now Bud and I enjoy our family gatherings most of all. The children all come to our house, and the grandchildren come and bring their boyfriends and girlfriends. We usually have twenty-eight to thirty eating with us on holidays. Our lives are gauged by having all of our children together from time to time. I don't know which stage of parenting is the most enjoyable; each one just seems to get better and better.

Vicki Rockett
Former schoolteacher and real estate agent
Full-time wife and mother of two children: Russell, seven,
   and Ryan, five
(Jean Rockett's daughter-in-law)

Unlike Dale's mother and father, who got married very young, Dale and I got married later in life. He was thirty-three, and I was twenty-nine. We both had careers before we married, and we had each lived alone and knew how to keep house and take care of our personal needs. Keeping the house clean after we got married just wasn't a problem for us. Jean had trained her son well; he has never been one to leave his clothing lying around. I've never had to pick up after him.

Dale and I both wanted children, and we are sharing in the responsibilities of raising them. They truly are "our" children.

My mother-in-law and I have quite a contrast: She worked when it wasn't popular for mothers to work, and forty years later, I'm staying at home when it isn't popular for mothers to stay home. The reason that I don't work is to be with my children. When I was young, all my friends played with Barbie dolls, but I always wanted to play with baby dolls. I have always wanted to be a mother, and when I got to be one, I wanted it to be on a full-time basis. We have made sacrifices for me to stay at home. Our house is very crowded now, and if I worked we could get a larger one; but right now it is more important for me to be at home. Next year when Ryan starts to school, I may take another look at working, but not now.

☙

I stay busy supporting the children in all of their activities. I know working mothers do the same, but I don't know how. I volunteer as room mother at Russell's school, and both he and I enjoy my doing it.

☙

Just sitting and watching the boys play and seeing how much they enjoy each other is something very special I wouldn't want to miss. After they've had their baths at night, said their prayers, and have been tucked into bed, I look at them and think what a wonderful gift children are.

☙

The children and I make things that we play with. Last week we made television cameras out of boxes. I try to give each of the boys special attention so neither feels a need to compete for my time. I think this is one reason why they enjoy each other so much.

☙

I didn't send either of the boys to preschool, and I'm very happy about that decision. Russell does very well in school, and if I had sent him to preschool, I'm sure I would have thought his performance was due to his prior preparation. Ryan is rhyming words and is learning quickly also without the preschool experience. I think children get a lot of security from home, without pressure. I think they need those years that are pressure free.

---- ☙ ----

Ann Stricklin
Women's retreat chairperson; former schoolteacher
Wife; mother of two adult children: Art, twenty-nine, and Cliff, twenty-six

Ever since our boys were infants, Gil and I have prayed that when the time came they would meet and marry wonderful Christian girls, and God was faithful in answering our prayers. This past year both of them married beautiful, Christian girls.

When the boys were young and Gil was traveling all over the world with the Billy Graham Crusades, we would keep a large world map posted on the wall. When Gil moved from spot to spot, we put a pin in the map to mark where he was at that time. This helped the boys stay in touch with their father when he wasn't home. We would always pray for him, and the boys could kind of visualize where he was. Gil was very good about sending tapes back, and I think this helped keep us close.

If God has given a parent a job to do, I believe He compensates and there is no damage to the child. Gil had a job that he had been called to do and he couldn't be with the boys all the time; but God could be a Father. When Gil was home, he was definitely involved in everything. I was fortunate in that I could be consistent in being home with the children all the time. Through the years, we have been very thankful that we both have a very good relationship with the boys.

When we were first married and Gil was in the Air Force, God taught me to be very dependent on Him. We were stationed in Greenville, South Carolina, and Gil was sent to the Antarctic for three months. I was teaching school, so I couldn't return to my home fifteen hundred miles away. Since I didn't have Gil or my family, I had to learn to be dependent on God.

Someone has said that the greatest gift you give to your children is that the mother loves the father and the father loves the mother. When that happens, the children feel secure and don't have to worry.

When Art was a baby, Gil was in the seminary, and it was necessary for me to work. I taught school in Fort Worth, and we had a wonderful baby-sitter who kept Art. My mother lived in Fort Worth also, and she helped out a lot. After Cliff was born, I did not resume my career. I was always at home when Art and Cliff got home from school. I think this is so important.

Going to church was a real anchor for the boys as they grew up. They participated in everything, Sunday school, choir, Royal Ambassadors. It is so important for children to be involved in the life of a church. When the boys were little, we read Bible stories to them and Gil would act out the plots. The boys loved all the action. We hardly ever put them to bed without a story.

We always traveled as a family, usually packed into some little car. I remember us driving a Volkswagen from coast to coast, and I would read stories out loud to the boys as they hung over the front seat. Mile after mile, Gil would drive and I would read. I tried to get a book that matched where we were going. When we went to the Grand Canyon, I read *Friday of the Grand Canyon,* and when we went to the East, I read a book about slaves in Massachusetts called *Venture for Freedom.* The boys' favorite books were the books I'd read on trips. Reading books to children is important whether they are Christian books, fun books, or just good books. It gives them a love of books, and also it creates a closeness. When they are little, you hold them close as you read.

It is important to find some niche that each child can be successful in, and really zero in on it. We all need to feel successful at something.

Traditions are so important, and celebrations are a part of those traditions. We celebrate everything, even down to Groundhog Day. I keep a roll of butcher paper for the sole purpose of making signs and banners for celebrations. Anything that mothers can do with children to build memories is so important.

Home needs to be a sanctuary for children. They need to be able to unload and have someone listen. Through the years, any time one of the boys would come in from a date, I'd always get up and meet him and we'd talk. Sometimes it was really hard because I would be very sleepy, but I'd always get up. It is important to let children know that you have time for them, no matter what time of the day it is. You are there to listen, not to judge, but to listen.

In raising children, you do the very best you can, you trust the Lord, and you never cease to pray for them, no matter what. Gil and I prayed over our children's cribs and we continued to pray with and for them all through the years. Gil keeps a prayer diary, and he writes down what he is praying for at the moment. It is interesting to see all the things that have been prayed about over the years.

I think being a mother is the greatest career a woman can have. I loved being a mother, but that doesn't mean that I didn't do other things. I was very busy as the boys were growing up, but I always tried to put down any project I was doing when they came home.

Nancy Terrell
Certified Public Accountant
Wife; mother of one child: Katie Beth, two

I worked for one of the "big ten" accounting firms until Katie Beth was born. I now work two days a week in an accounting office, and I run my own business out of our home. I just got another new client which will require twenty hours a week of my time. The stress is building.

Childcare is always a big consideration. I've had Katie Beth in several different places, and I've learned that the most expensive care is not always the best care. Brian helps a lot. If he didn't I don't know how I'd make it.

Society puts so much pressure on us mothers. It always seems to tell us we should be doing more. I am very busy all the time, but I keep thinking I should be doing more. I tell myself not to think like this, but I don't take my own advice very well.

In college, anything Brian and I tried for, we were able to do. Out of five thousand graduates at Texas A&M, Brian was the outstanding graduate. I did a lot on campus, too, and had ten job offers when I graduated. Brian and I both felt invincible. But we have found the real world can really kick you around. Getting high-power jobs when you graduate can put you under a lot of pressure. I wish I could have learned while I was going through college how hard life can be. It really came as such a shock.

Katie Beth has been such an easy child. She goes to bed at eight o'clock every night, and then Brian and I do more work. I've turned down new clients this month because I just can't take any more work right now.

If parents asked me about daycare, I'd tell them to make surprise visits to the centers and look for themselves. I've visited a lot of different places, and some of them certainly didn't live up to their reputations. It's very hard to find good places that will take a child just two or three days a week. They want a full-time child in that slot. Childcare is definitely the number-one problem for working mothers.

Joan Pennington
Former secretary
Wife; mother of three adult children: De De, Mary Grace, and Melissa
Grandmother of one child

Before we were married, Frank and I had talked about wanting five children; but then we were married for nine years and didn't have a baby. I had wanted a child desperately, and we were so happy when the adoption agency told us it had a little girl for us. Five months after De De arrived, I went to the doctor because I was gaining so much weight from being at home and eating so much—so I thought. What a shock it was when the doctor told me that if I waited four more months, I would lose the weight that was causing me concern. I was five months pregnant! Our second daughter arrived two weeks early; so before De De was nine months old, she had a little sister. Then a year later, I was pregnant with another baby. When Melissa was born, De De was not yet three years old. Three children under three years of age were ours to cherish and love.

My husband was so very patient and helpful. He told me he didn't expect one thing of me except for us all "just to be there" when he got home at night. I was rather a relaxed person, and had never believed that a house had to be picture perfect; but how nice it was to have a husband who didn't expect the house to be clean or dinner to be prepared when he walked in. He really gave me permission to just plod along and do the best I could until the children got a little older. When he came in the door at night, he just took charge of the children and entertained them while I cooked dinner. He bathed them, washed their hair, and did everything they needed; it was such a tremendous help to me. It's so hard on women who have husbands who don't help, because when the children are tiny, it's a two-parent project. My husband changed diapers in an era when men didn't do that; but the children were out of diapers before he knew he wasn't supposed to change them!

Boys and girls should read all the books on parenting when they are in high school, because once you have children, you don't have time to read how to parent.

I was a preacher's kid who loved the church. It was my favorite place to be, and still is. Frank loves the church, too. When the children started to school, though, he said, "I don't care how involved you get in church; but I just feel you should be at home at three o'clock every day when the kids get off the school bus." I always made a real effort to be home every day when they arrived; but if I happened not to be, they were welcomed next door by our good neighbors.

God gave me a wonderful gift when the children were small. A family with four children moved in next door to us when our oldest one was around four, and soon a fifth child was born into their home. These children had a mother who was a saint. Joan Hill was a person who put her family first, and there was no question about it. I had always tried to be somewhat organized and have some semblance of neatness in the house, but these things didn't bother Joan at all. I will never forget she'd pile all the clean clothes from her huge wash onto her kitchen table. She would stop right in the middle of folding this stack of laundry and bake cookies because it would be nearly time for her children to get home from school. Everyone in the neighborhood would gather at her house because she was so friendly and so nice. She baked wonderful bread, and she'd have all the children in the neighborhood waiting for a slice. My children just loved going to her house, and she was really better to me than a sister could be.

I feel that God sent her to me when I needed a friend like that who had her priorities in order. It was no surprise to me that her children grew up to be such a great family. She taught me so much about materialism and what is really important. It didn't matter if there were laundry on the table. What really mattered was the love in that home. She taught me that when a mother has peace of mind, she passes it on to her children.

Another gift from God is grandparents. Frank's parents would take one child at a time home with them. They lived in Waco, Texas, and we lived in Houston; there was a restaurant half-way between the two cities where we'd meet to transfer a child from one car to another. My parents were and are just as wonderful to the children as Frank's parents are.

When children are teenagers, it is so important to help them look the very best they can, whether that means getting braces on the teeth, going to the dermatologist, styling the hair, or buying clothes. Some people think this is shallow, but teenagers need to really feel good about themselves. Looking good helps them to feel good.

One of our girls had a teacher at school who was just verbally cruel to the children in her class. Her words really hurt one of our daughters, so we started praying for this woman. Every night my daughter and I would get down on our knees to pray for her, and gradually we began to see this teacher change.

During her teenage years, one of our daughters went through a period of rebellion and pulling away from the family. We had always had a close-knit family up until this time, and this change in our daughter brought us great pain. Frank and I had raised all of our girls in the church, and having problems was just something we had not anticipated. We searched our own hearts to see if maybe we could have done something to cause this rebellion; but quite honestly, we are still baffled. Frank and I had never treated this daughter any differently than the other two. We tried everything: praying, talking, making rules more strict or less strict, counseling, taking trips; but nothing seemed to improve. She wanted to quit school, but we insisted that she remain until she graduated. We told her if she would stay at home until she finished the twelfth grade, we would rent an apartment for her to go to college. We knew we had to release her, but we would always pray that someday things would be better for her and for us. Releasing her was the right thing to do. She no longer had to live by our rules, and there was no reason to rebel. She is married now to a wonderful man, and they seem very happy. I hear so many mothers say they wonder why their child, who has been so loved and cared for, decides to rebel during the teenage years. We don't really have an answer, but we just have to trust God to work out the problems in His time and His way.

Armi Lizardi
Newspaper and magazine photographer
Wife; mother of three children: James, twenty-three; Lisa, twenty-one; and Mindy, nineteen

My own mother worked when I was growing up, but I had a grandmother who was always there for me. I never felt alone. My mother was a beautician, and she always wanted me to look just right when I went somewhere. I will never forget the way she put my hair into French braids. Oh, how I hated those braids! She'd also dress me in starched pinafore dresses. She wasn't just concerned about my outward appearance, though; she wanted me always to be kind and respectful.

Since my mother worked, I grew up knowing that we all pitched in around the house. This included my brother, as well. Whoever got home first would start dinner. My dad loved to cook and he'd help, too.

After I was married and had preteenage children, my father had a stroke and was paralyzed. My husband and I both agreed that we should move my mother and father into our home. It is amazing how many of our friends didn't think we should do that, but it was the best thing we could have done for our own children. They would come home from school, and my father, sitting in his wheelchair, would tell them all these wonderful stories about his life. If the children hadn't had the opportunity to come home and be with my father, help feed him, and push him around in his wheelchair, they would have missed a whole lot of closeness. James, especially, became very close to his grandfather. When we were making funeral arrangements after my father died, it was James who was able to give all the details about his grandfather's life. I am real proud of my children for their sensitivity to older people. They are caring and understanding, and I know they learned that from having my parents in our home for that period of time.

Our children are living at home now, and the same people who criticized us for having my parents live with us are telling us now that the children shouldn't live at home;

but that's all right. We are thoroughly enjoying them as adults, and our arrangement works out beautifully for all of us. We know they won't be with us permanently, but we are thankful for these added years that we can all enjoy being a family living and working together.

With my job, I see all kinds of things that happen to young people in this day and time, and I know the difference a supportive family can make in their lives. I think every kid deserves to be a part of such a family.

Dawn Brainard
Data operations analyst for an engineering company
Wife; mother of one child: Steven, two

For as long as I can remember, all I have ever wanted was to just get married and have babies. Now I am married and I have a child and one on the way; but I also have something else. I have a full-time job. I would love to stay at home with my son who is two, and with the baby who is soon to be born; but it isn't possible for me to do that at this time. My mother worked and I was raised by baby-sitters, and I didn't want that for my own children. I wanted to stay at home, bake cookies, and be a good mom. I am constantly figuring and refiguring the bills to see when I can quit and be home full time. It's a goal that Mark and I talk about all the time.

Steven was only seven weeks old when I went back to work, and I cried and cried when I had to leave him. My third day back at work, I just burst into tears, and said, "I can't do it. I just can't do it." Unfortunately, I made such a big deal of staying at home that it made Mark feel inadequate. Unintentionally, I was making him feel that he couldn't provide for us, and that was creating a problem for him. When I realized that, I totally backed off. I have to accept the fact that I can't change things and that I have to work now. Besides, I know that Steven is being well taken care of. We just have to make the most of our situation.

⁂

I want to spend as much time with my children as I can, because they aren't kids very long. When they start to school, I want to be a room mother. My mother could never do those things because she worked. She'd bake cupcakes, and I'd take them to the baby-sitter and then on to school, but she wasn't able to come to school herself.

⁂

Being a mom is what I really want; yet I am kind of torn because I want some things for myself, too. I wouldn't mind having a job part-time where I could have a little time away from the house and be with adults.

⁂

Steven is with the baby-sitter from before seven in the morning to after four in the afternoon, and sometimes I feel like she contributes more to him than I do. When we are home, I just want to be with him, to do things for him, to contribute to him, too. But I think Steven is more fortunate than a lot of children. Because Mark and I work at the same place, we both drop him off at the sitter's and we both pick him up. We live about an hour from our work; but I purposefully found a baby-sitter just a few blocks from work, so that we could all spend that travel time together.

⁂

My father was a cross-country truck driver, and my mother had to do everything for us. She had total responsibility when my father was away, but my situation is entirely different. Mark helps me do everything. He is so self-sufficient. If a button comes off his shirt, he sews it back on. There is nothing around the house that he can't do.

We take Steven to a family-home baby-sitter, and the woman is just wonderful with children. She keeps her own grandchildren, as well as other kids, and she does so much for all of them. Spending one-on-one time with each child is important to her, and she teaches them so many things. I don't have to worry about her just putting the children in the back yard and forgetting about them like the baby-sitter did when I was a child. I can still remember that as soon as my mother dropped me off, that woman used to say, "Get in the back yard." She'd shut the door, and we were out there all day. Having had this experience and knowing what types of baby-sitters are out there, I thought finding a good one was going to be an impossible task. I was wrong. The woman we found is excellent. I couldn't ask for anyone better.

Working is like a Catch 22. I work because we need the money, but yet so much of that money goes to the baby-sitter. Some people say, "Why bother working, if it takes so much of your salary just to pay for childcare?" I answer by saying, "But you don't understand. We need what's left over. We can't get by without it."

I'd like to start my maternity leave a few weeks before the new baby is born just to spend some time with Steven, because it will never be just the two of us again. I'd be cutting time off the other end of my six weeks' maternity leave; but I don't think it will be as hard to leave a new baby this time. I have confidence in our sitter, and I know now that leaving a child can work out all right. I also know I have to. I would never again put Mark through what I did last time. I was so selfish, because I was completely caught up in my emotions and in what I wanted.

Sometimes I will look out the window at work and see a mother strolling her baby down the sidewalk, and I think, *I wish I could do that. I wish I could take my son to the park.* I tell myself I'll do it on the weekend, but those two days are filled with so many chores that must be done. Mark and I have all the housework to do, the grocery shopping to take care of, and all the clothes to get ready for the next week. Anything that I don't get done just puts me that much farther behind.

Steven provides all our entertainment. After we've left him all week, we don't want to leave him again with someone and go out. But we're fortunate because Mark and I do have our private time together during the week. Since we work at the same place, we eat our lunch together every day and we talk. Sometimes, we take our lunch and go out to the park. People often ask us how we can spend every lunch hour together, but we love it. I can't be with my son during the day, but I can be with my husband. We can't have it all.

Caroline Brainard
Wife and mother of seven adult children: Patrick, Mark,
   Chris, Paul, Laura, Nancy, and Cari Ann
Grandmother of five children
(Dawn Brainard's mother-in-law)

After my husband and I had our four boys, we thought we'd like to have a little girl; so when our pastor announced at Wednesday-night services that two little girls were in need of a home, we decided to meet them. We made that initial visit and brought home these two little girls, ages three and five. We didn't know anything about getting a foster-care license; but we immediately started the process. It took about six months before we were licensed; but the girls were allowed to stay with us during that time. Two years later, I gave birth to another child, a little girl we named Cari Ann.

⁂

I thought all the children should know how to do housework. When they grew up and left my house, I wanted them to know how to cook, clean house, mend, wash, and iron. My father had done those things; my husband grew up doing them. And I wanted my children to know how, too.

⁂

When the children were growing up, our social life was centered around the church activities. Church has always been important to our family, and we have gone to the same one for many years.

⁂

My kitchen was always open to those who wanted to go in and prepare food for themselves. I cooked meals; but if the children wanted anything at any other time, they prepared it themselves. They all learned to cook well, and two of my sons are excellent cooks. One loves to prepare gourmet food, and also is a wonderful baker.

⁂

Since the children are grown, Dave and I often rent a large condominium during the summer and invite them to come and spend time with us in Catalina or someplace like that. It's a wonderful way to spend time with the children and the grandchildren.

⁂

The majority of the birthdays in our family fall between August and December, so we have group birthday parties. Getting everyone together for these celebrations is another way of keeping us all in close touch with one another.

I try to be accommodating with my children's families having their own holiday celebrations at Christmas and Thanksgiving; I tell them to pick a day when everyone can come to our house. Last year, we had our Thanksgiving celebration on Saturday because that was the day everyone could come. I've found that it really doesn't matter if we celebrate at my house on the exact day of the holiday. The main thing is that we all get together sometime during that week.

Katie Fujitaki
Beautician and co-owner of a beauty salon
Wife; mother of two children: Ronald, twenty-seven, and Margaret, twenty-five

I came to the United States from Japan in 1961, and my two children were born in this country. I stayed at home with my children until my daughter started to school, and then I worked at a part-time job.

I worked only part time because my husband wanted me to be home when the children came home. Every day, I was home at least five minutes before they arrived.

I had worked in Japan as a cosmetologist for fifteen years before I came to the United States. My work was divided into three areas: I traveled all over Japan with beauty shows, I taught in a beauty school, and I worked in a beauty salon. My father was an educator, and growing up I had always planned to go to college. But World War II changed all of my plans. We lost everything during the war, and sometimes there wasn't even enough food to eat. When the war was over, my father told me that I should go to beauty school and learn a skill. I cried and cried because I had always wanted to be a schoolteacher.

                                                      ∽

When I was five years old, I had a kindergarten teacher who made a lasting impression on my life. She was a Christian missionary with blonde hair and blue eyes, and she taught me all about Jesus and all about America. I started thinking then that one day I wanted to go to the United States.

                                                      ∽

Some of the things that happened to me in Miss Cadeback's kindergarten class made such an impression that I remembered their importance when I was raising my own children. For example, at Christmas time, my kindergarten class put on a play about the birth of Jesus. I was chosen to be the bright star that led others to Christ's birthplace in Bethlehem. I wore a crown with a star and carried stars in my hand. As I walked backward down the aisle, holding the star up high, three boys dressed as the wise men followed me. Other children followed, playing the roles of shepherds and their sheep. On the stage around the nativity scene were children playing the roles of Mary and Joseph. There was also an angel on stage, and a light shone on this angel as if it were a light from my star. That was a moment I will never forget. I felt that I always wanted my life to be just like it was that night. I wanted to always be a shining star, no matter where I was. I wanted my light to shine on others and help them.

                                                      ∽

A goal was established in my life at that very young age. The goal was that I might help other people and that I might be a good person—a person just like Miss Cadeback. I didn't know then the importance of self-esteem in a child's life; but because of that night, I knew later when I was a parent how important it was for my children to have good self-esteem in their own lives. I also knew the value of their having goals for their lives.

My parents also influenced how I raised my own children. They were very strict, and they always made me follow the rules; but when I did something good, my parents always talked about this at family discussion time. I learned to respect my parents and other people. My father had a motto, and when I was raising my children, it became my motto, too. It read: In the morning, think of your goal. In the daytime, do your best. In the evening, be thankful and keep love in your heart.

My husband and I first met in high school; but he moved to the United States in 1950, and I didn't see him again until I came to this country in 1961. There were ten girls to every boy in Japan at that time, and it was very difficult to find a good husband. A friend of our family suggested that I marry this man who now lived in America. My parents agreed, and I was happy because I would be married to a good man, and I would live in a country where I had always wanted to be. My parents arranged the marriage, and I came to the United States all alone and got married. I have been very happy here with my husband and my two children. My children are grown now and both have finished college. My daughter is an accountant, and my son will graduate from dental school this year.

When my children started to preschool, I started to school, too. I first learned English, and then I started taking college courses, one at a time. I am still taking courses, and some year I plan to get my degree.

I think it is so important for mothers to stay at home with their children until they start to school. A young child needs to know a mother's love all during the day.

Beverly Goddard
Former schoolteacher
Wife; mother of two children: Sheryl, thirty-two, and Shauna, twenty-five
Grandmother of two children

As pastor and pastor's wife, my husband and I were always very busy in the church. We enjoyed our two girls so much, and so did the members of the congregation. Because we were at church so much of the time, the church membership became like an extended family to our children.

We felt like our children needed some activity that they could do on their own which wasn't just an extension of our church work. They both loved to sing and dance, so when they were quite young each girl started taking dance lessons. When they began, we felt like it was just a good physical activity, and we had no idea that they both would become so good at their lessons. The girls would eventually go on to perform nationally and internationally, each achieving her share of fame in concert work, television, and films. Our older daughter gave up her career at an early age to marry an internationally known rock star. They have had a fourteen-year, non-Hollywood-type marriage, and are the parents of two children. Our younger daughter is still going strong in her career, with only a four-year hiatus to get her bachelor's degree from UCLA. Currently, she is starring in a television show in Rome, Italy.

We have always told our girls that our greatest pride would be in their spiritual development, so we sought close family ties and bonding in the word of God. Bill and I feel that God should be first in our lives. Family should be second, and church work should be third. It appears to us that if this order is tampered with, resentment sets in. It's amazing how much church work can be accomplished when this order is adhered to.

We are still mothers when our children are grown, but we have to do things a little differently than when they were younger. I don't have the philosophy that you should just not say anything, because, after all, you are still a mother. You may not still be the prime decision maker; but just because they get grown doesn't mean you don't have opinions and you shouldn't have any input. You should have input; but it has to be done very, very carefully. Your adult children still have to know you have a brain in your head, and you have a thought, and that you still have a philosophy. It has to be very gentle guidance, and much more humble. You can't be filled with dictatorial powers. Instead, you need to be filled with humble suggestions.

Early on in our children's lives, we sought to define spiritual values. So many parents make the mistake of only being attentive to the physical, emotional, and intellectual needs of their children. The result is a spiritual vacuum in the child which develops quickly and early. The child will soon invent a god of his or her own. One mother I know found out her child's god was a combination of Superman and Mickey Mouse. Needless to say, she quickly enrolled him in a Bible study class. If parents really knew the heartache of not developing a child spiritually, they would be just as concerned about that area as they are about the child's general health and emotional well-being. If there is one thing that I could say to young mothers, it would be not only to look out for the physical and mental needs of their children, but to look out for the spiritual needs as well.

Parents also must develop themselves spiritually. It doesn't work to just try to develop the spiritual lives of the children without also thinking about the lives of the parents.

We decided that sometimes we would take a trip which involved only one parent and one child, with that child having the parent's undivided attention. It wasn't often that we did this, because most of the trips included all four of us. However, some of the one-parent, one-child trips are the ones the children, as adults today, remember the most.

I have often been asked how we reconcile two successful, performing daughters with our Christian faith. We have tried to teach each daughter how to be a Christian in a secular world. That is what every parent has to eventually teach, no matter what career the child goes into. The thing that I've always tried to strive for is wisdom for the children. If you read Proverbs, we see that this is a gift of God; but it's something we have to really seek in order to develop. Through wisdom comes discernment—learning right from wrong, learning what's good and what's not so good, learning what to approach and what to avoid. Once our children become Christians, we need to pray that they will have this wisdom so they can live their Christianity in a very secular world, no matter what their profession is. Struggles in a secular world produce Christian character for the child of God. That is what we have always tried to teach our daughters, and prayed would happen for them.

God has been faithful to answer our prayers. Both daughters are "born anew" in Christ. One grandchild had this same spiritual experience last year. Both daughters attend church and Bible study regularly. And our rock-star son-in-law? Well, go to the church he attends on Sunday, and you will see him bowing his head and worshiping with his family. "Seek ye first the kingdom of God . . . and all these things shall be added unto you" (Matt. 6:33, KJV).

Mary Ida Phair
Retired high-school librarian
Wife; mother of two adult children: Rob and Randy
Grandmother of three children

I have often said that my life has consisted of twenty-year segments. The first twenty years I was growing up and going to school. I was married at age twenty-one, and the next twenty years I was raising our two boys. Twenty years later, I finished my college education, and at age forty-two I started to work as a high-school librarian. After remaining at that one job for twenty years, I retired in 1982, and I am now on my next twenty years. Currently, I'm working part-time in a private-school library and doing volunteer work several places in the community.

Timing in life is what makes the difference, and not pressuring a situation if it doesn't seem right. I was fortunate because I didn't have to choose between my family and my career; I've gotten to enjoy both without having to sacrifice either one.

Probably the most fun time of my life was the twenty-year segment when I was rearing the boys. At that time in our society, mothers didn't have to work because two incomes were not necessary to support the household. We didn't have to choose between a profession and a family. I didn't have my librarian credentials at that time, but I would not have chosen to work then, anyway. No one worked that I knew of, unless there was a real financial need; I was fortunate that my husband had a good job and provided for us.

We had a large back yard, and our house was the gathering place for all the kids in the neighborhood. I thought that it was important to participate with the children, so I became involved in their activities.

I think a woman particularly has to have something that belongs especially to her, something that comes from inside, but which isn't too obvious so as not to cause a woman to sacrifice her role as a wife and mother. It is a hidden desire that is so strong in her that she finds a way to express it—maybe a kind of label that means something special to her. I see many women my age who are sort of unidentified or a nonentity—not that a woman has to do anything spectacular; but she has to have something that belongs especially to her. The women I know who are the most satisfied see a need for this. It has to be an ongoing thing, nothing that is static. I think that is what keeps women alive, animated, and fun. Women should be this way for the sake of their children. Everyone enjoys being around a woman who is alive and filled with energy.

Teaching children to be truthful is so important. My husband always said to our boys, "You come home and tell us the truth, and no matter what happens, we will always back you up." We stressed this to our boys, and they remembered it. We always tried to be completely honest with them, also.

Parents need to see what is really important to their children, and they need to make sacrifices for them to have those things. I don't believe that children should have to work after school, make minimal wages, and miss out on the important happenings of school life. Just remember, timing is so important. Sometimes you have to do something for one of your children right at that time because if you wait, it may be too late.

Bonnie Bear
Public-school nurse
Wife; mother of three children: Brian, twenty-three; Lisa, twenty-one; and Kevin, nineteen

When the children were small, I worked part time at the hospital on the eleven-to-seven shift. After they started to school, I deliberately chose to go into school nursing because it fit into my children's school calendar. When they were five, seven, and eight, I drove a hundred miles a day to work and then went to school two nights a week. Mothers do what is necessary.

I always considered it extremely important to make personal contact with my children's teachers. Establishing a close relationship with a teacher will be one of the most critical things you do for your child.

Men are task oriented. Women need to target their home-care needs to their husbands for maximum cooperation. However, I don't think the man should be made into a housewife.

When I got home from work, I would take the food out of the Crock-Pot, and then I'd supervise the children's studying. Getting homework done was something that was stressed in our home, but I was there to help if needed.

I let the children be themselves. I've never tried to put them into a mold. I think that it is important to let them develop their own personalities. Let the child come to you. Be child centered and not mother centered. The child needs you and will come to you when he or she needs to.

Some mothers are very competitive, and they try to sign up their children for everything. They program their kids. I don't believe this is the right thing to do.

Mothers need to relax and not be uptight. Believe in your children, and expect them to follow the rules.

Debbie Quinn
Christian radio-station producer
Wife; mother of five children: Kevin, eight; Jonathan, seven; Charles, six; and Adam and Benjamin, four

I went back to college when the twins were two years old, and I am majoring in radio broadcasting. Right now I am working part time and going to school full time. I am also a full-time mother.

My busy schedule works for me because my husband is so good to help with the boys. We've also trained the children to pick up after themselves. We not only tell them to do this, but we set the example by picking up after ourselves.

Each child is a special part of my life, and he is aware of it. I have a date with each of my sons once a month. I let the child do something with me first, like go shopping, and then I do whatever he wants to do.

Communicating with your spouse is so very important. Even as busy as I am, once a week my husband and I go out together so we can talk.

Mothers need to use their time wisely. It is so much easier to do this when you are organized. I couldn't get through my day if I didn't organize as I go along. As a mother of five, I need to save as many steps as possible.

I have always believed in having obtainable goals for myself and my family. Some of these goals should be wide so there will be room for flexibility. My life is centered around my priorities. God is first and my family is second. Every day we have ten minutes of Bible study.

I think when you are playing with your children, you should do the things they like to do. My boys like to make pies, especially pumpkin pies, and we do that together. We take walks, also.

Judy Shrader
Hospital critical-care nurse
Wife; mother of four children: Tiffany, twelve; Teddy, six; Scotty, two; and Christy, nine months

I work in a hospital two days a week from 7 A.M. to 7:30 P.M., and this schedule seems to work out best for our family. Because we have an au pair living in our home, I am able to be gone all day.

Two of our children were born to us and two are foster children. They are all equally precious to us. By being a foster mom, I feel that I am making a difference in the life of a child who needs someone to step in and be supportive and loving.

⁓

I don't think there is any such thing as a woman's role. My husband steps in and does everything I do. Ed bonds with the children, and he knows their needs and their wants. In the mornings, he gets up and gets them to school.

⁓

Children must get quality care while the mother is away, not a hit-and-miss thing. I think au pairs are wonderful because they live in your home and become a part of the family. They love the children, too, and when the mother goes to work, she leaves the children with someone who really cares about them.

⁓

I think employers should be more supportive of mothers, especially when the children are small. There are times when the mother must be with a child, and the employers need to understand this.

⁓

I do all kinds of things with our children, from taking walks to signing them up to be extras in movies. Mothers need to look around and see what is available in their communities for the children. Life is really a lot of fun with children in the home if you make it that way.

Ann Bengford
Hospital nurse
Wife; mother of six children: Pat, thirty-one; Tony, twenty-nine; Kathryn, twenty-six; Christopher, twenty-two; Phillip, nineteen; and Timothy, sixteen

I have always considered my husband and the children my career, and nursing my profession. What I mean is my husband and children are my number-one priority, but when I walk out the door to go on duty, I give my full attention to my profession. When the children were little, they knew they were not to call me at work unless it was an emergency. The number where I could be reached was always on the chalkboard in the kitchen.

When I roll out of bed in the morning, I say to myself, *This is the best day I'm going to have.* For twenty-five years, when the children were growing up, I went to Mass every morning. I had more energy and pep when I prepared at church early in the mornings.

We sent our kids to parochial schools for the first eight years. It was hard financially to do that, but it was worth every penny. The good Lord provided the money all those years. When the last child finished eighth grade, we had a big party in the back yard. We made a fire and burned all the tuition books that we'd accumulated over the twenty-five years our children had been going to that school.

We baked our own bread and made our own cakes and pies. I canned jams and jellies and did all the washing and ironing. All the kids can bake a pie. At Christmas time, Ken always purchases a box of apples from the produce market, and all the children come into the kitchen to help me peel. Then we all bake apples pies together. I've worked hard; but it is a joy. To cook is therapy.

I would say to young mothers, "Laugh a lot, even when you don't feel like laughing. Find some joy in everything." Children broaden your horizon. They keep you young. They are a joy to the world.

⌒

I always got up and made sure the kids had a decent breakfast. I've been told that kids can get up and get their own breakfast, but I think that it is important to see to it that they have a good meal before they take off for school.

⌒

Ken is a schoolteacher, a great support, and a good father. We fulfilled the needs of the children, but the wants did not always get filled. To keep up with the Joneses was never considered.

⌒

Before Pat was born, I worked in a doctor's office; but with each of my children I stayed home for the first six months and nursed the baby. When they started drinking from a cup, I'd go back to work, but usually I just worked part time on the three-to-eleven shift. We always managed to have one parent in the home with the children. When the children all got into school, I went back to work full time.

⌒

I was never concerned about the house being neat. It was clean enough to be healthy, and dirty enough to be lived in.

⌒

Ken and I raised six kids with only one bath in the house. The shower was completely enclosed, so if someone had to go to the bathroom in an emergency, he or she could do that. This family didn't know any different. We made do.

Kathy Waterman
Teacher; district coordinator for drug-abuse programs
Wife; mother of three children: Bryan, thirteen; Mark, ten;
  and Scott, seven

Jim and I met while we were both attending Westmont College. We were married in 1974, and he went on to the seminary to prepare for the ministry. I taught high-school physical education and coached track. When Jim got out of the seminary, he accepted a position as associate pastor with a church in San Luis Obispo. I stayed home with our first child and helped Jim in his work. I didn't work for the next nine years. We basically had a team ministry, working a lot with college students.

After some very productive and happy years in his first position, Jim got a call to serve as the pastor for a small church in central California. By this time, we had two children. Moving to a small town and living on a dirt road was a real change for me, and it took some adjustment. I didn't work outside the home; but I did develop a women's circle within the church. Bible Study Fellowship met my needs at that time, basically for cultivating friendships. A third son was born when we were in the small-church ministry.

I wasn't a typical pastor's wife. I didn't play the piano and do the things one usually associates with a wife in that role. I became involved with women's athletics in the 1960s when it really wasn't the thing to do. Every weekend when I was in high school, my father drove me a hundred miles to train with my team. I was one of the first women in the United States to run the mile competitively. Later, I traveled all over the country and became tenth in the nation in that event. It was a good experience and has made a real impression on me as to what women can do today.

It bothers me when I go to Christian conferences and only men are up front speaking. I feel very capable women are often pushed aside in our churches. That is a real issue to me. I feel that a lot of professional women are not being reached today because they don't see women in leadership roles in the churches and they don't relate to it.

I love my three sons dearly; but I'd also really like to have a daughter. I have always known I'd be a mother, but I've always known that I wanted to do something else, too.

When the children were nine, six, and three, my husband and I felt that he should go back to seminary and get a degree in clinical psychology. He was a wonderful preacher, but he felt God was calling him to use other gifts, too. He was accepted right away in a program that was very difficult to get into, so we felt God had to be opening doors for us. I was happy about our new move; but I also knew that I must go back to work full time.

Jim and I changed roles when he entered the seminary the second time. I became the breadwinner, and he provided moral support at home. He arranged his schedule so he could be at home when the children came in from school. When I went back to work, our youngest child was able to attend a preschool which Fuller Theological Seminary had just started to offer. I obtained a job teaching physical education and health at a junior high school. During that time I helped write an AIDS curriculum for the district. After two years, I moved to a district closer to my home and took a job teaching physical science at a high school. Working at a job near my home and not having to spend time on the freeway made a lot of difference to me.

Jim became very good with the meals. I had always been pretty possessive with my kitchen, but I realized I needed to change and allow Jim to do his part. I've been amazed at how creative he has become in the kitchen.

I see young couples today invest a lot into their children but fail to put that same energy into maintaining the husband-wife relationship. I feel it is very important to make the effort to get away together. We go to matinees instead of the more expensive evening movies. We also eat at the restaurants that have early-bird specials. When Jim and I go away for the weekend, we stay at economical hotels. We often eat cheese and crackers for lunch so we can have a nice dinner out.

I consider myself a real bargain hunter and this has always helped us, especially when I did not work outside the home. I watch the sales, and if I see something early in the season, I wait until it goes on sale. I like to wear stylish clothes, but I have to wait until they are marked down. Living on a pastor's salary and then a teaching salary has been a challenge.

I think women in the 1980s were told they could have it all. And I think this produced a lot of angry young women—Christian women included. I think it is very hard to work full time, be a full-time mother, and have a husband working full time. Last year, all three boys were on different Little League teams and we went to some sixty-six ball games. Jim and I have worked real hard to keep everything together; but I think half the time, we feel like we're about ready to fall off the mountain.

While Jim has been in the seminary and I've been working, we have started a Stephen's ministry in our own church. Stephen's ministry is training adults to be caregivers and then matching the adults to others in crisis. We were able to continue this one night a week for three years. The Stephen's ministry was a real self-esteem builder for me. It was God reassuring me that I could serve Him in teaching adults. We worked with a lot of great people, and they were very reaffirming.

The four years Jim has been in the seminary this second time could have been very miserable; but they turned out to be a period of personal growth, good experiences for the children, achievement for Jim, and new professional experiences for me. I've learned a lot from being a working mother.

One thing I have tried to do is to have special time with each child once or twice every two weeks. One place that was fun for us was to go to McDonald's and get a coke and fries and then go to a cemetery and take a walk and talk. The cemetery was quiet and just being there raised topics and questions concerning death. Lately when I've been home at night alone with the boys, we have taken walks. At first my older son said, "Mom, that's old-fashioned." But now I really think he doesn't mind it.

This past year, I directed a drug and alcohol program for four high schools, and I really enjoyed the challenge. But just when my career is really beginning to blossom, I must leave. Jim received his Ph.D. a few months ago, and we are moving across country at the end of summer so he can complete his clinical internship on the East Coast. Making changes and being flexible are things working mothers must do.

Martha Sanford
Professor of nursing
Wife; mother of four children: Brian, thirty; Allison, twenty-nine; Raleigh, twenty-eight; and Madeleine, eighteen
Grandmother of five

I worked only part time until the youngest of my first three children was in first grade. I was one of those "washing-machine nurses." If you needed a new washer, you went back to work. I worked part time for another reason, too. I needed the intellectual stimulation. I remember one year I worked four hours an evening twice a week. I enjoyed nursing, and it filled a need both financially and intellectually.

When my husband lost his job and I had to go back to work full time, it was quite an adjustment for me. Coming from a traditional Christian background, the first thing I did was say to God, "Lord, I know you can find my husband a job." But He didn't. I couldn't understand why my prayers were not being answered; but I did realize that I had no other alternative than to go to work full time. During this time, the demand for engineers was at all-time low, and my husband didn't find a job for two years. Now I see my working as something that helped shape our future in a very positive way.

When our fourth child was born, I had to continue working full time. Fortunately, I found an older woman who kept the baby while I was away. I usually got home by 3:30, and the older three children arrived about the same time. They enjoyed playing with the baby while I cooked dinner, washed clothes, and cleaned house, but I wasn't getting to enjoy her. So I assigned chores for each of us to do, thus freeing me to enjoy my baby, too.

In 1975, nineteen years after I had graduated from nursing school, I went back to college to get my degree. Madeleine, my youngest child, was two years old, and I was working full time. In ten years I went from having a diploma in nursing to having a doctorate degree. I made the decision that since it was necessary for me to work, I wanted to get the education and job that I most enjoyed. I worked full time until the last two years of the doctorate program, and then I worked part time again.

I believe young mothers need intellectual stimulation. In the years before I went back to work full time, my husband and I went to a Great Books discussion group. We did this nine months out of the year for seven years. I think parents who keep up with their own education will have a better balanced life. We often discussed these books at the dinner table, and the children benefited from our discussions. I found this out later from the kids, themselves.

When women have a career, I feel they do not experience the empty-nest syndrome when their children leave home.

I think it is important to live close to the grandchildren. Kids need their grandparents, and parents need a break from the day-to-day stress.

Three of our children have college degrees, and the youngest one will enter college this year. I believe going back to college, myself, helped motivate them to know the value of education. I think the part-time jobs the kids had while they were in school also helped them realize they needed credentials to get better jobs. Working helps the kids learn how to get along with people, as well.

Our family has a four-generation reunion every year. The children have been able to see how important their heritage is. Al sends out a newsletter to 125 family members twice a year, and this helps keep us connected. I feel that family reunions and newsletters are so important to show the young people continuity, so they sense a feeling of extended family.

Even though I worked and went to school, we always went to church as a family. The kids had a lot of freedom growing up, but they had friends who went to church. Church and school kept them occupied.

I think most women who work do it out of necessity, whether it comes from within them, as something they have to do, or it is a financial necessity. The rewards come from contributing to the growth and development of the family. Everyone works together to get needs met. I think the stereotype of the woman working just because she has a big salary and important career is very rare. I think most women work because they have to work.

I want my children to know the Bible is the wisdom of the ages and something they can accept as a standard for their lives. If they know this, they don't have to experience all of life's trials all over again.

Della Burns
Former schoolteacher
Widow; mother of three children: Ruth, seventy-six; Alice (deceased); and William, sixty-nine
Seven grandchildren, fourteen great-grandchildren, and five great-great-grandchildren

I was born in a log cabin near Rice, Kansas, on December 27, 1892. I graduated from college and taught school for one year before getting married. My husband and I lived on a farm, and I helped stack hay, shuck corn, and milk cows. Three children were born to us, two girls and a boy.

When the children were quite small, I lost my husband, and I had to go back to work. Besides teaching, I also worked in the hospital as a nurse's aide. I really enjoyed that work, because I had wanted to be a registered nurse — but my parents had wanted me to be a teacher.

I never had any trouble with my children. I think mothers should talk to their children and listen to their needs. I always took my children to church, and I taught them right from wrong.

I remarried in 1941. My second husband and I moved to town because of his health. I then had the opportunity to be superintendent for the cradle-roll department. About twelve years later, after he passed away, I worked at a girls' industrial school in Kansas.

In November 1973, I moved to California. My son insisted that I make the move. He said that he'd pay all the expenses, and if I didn't like it he would move me back. He wanted me to be near him and one of my daughters. My grandson drove my car to California for me.

I accepted Christ at an early age, and church activities have always been important in my life. When I moved to California, I joined a local church, and for years I've baked bread for the communion services. I've also taught bread-baking classes, and even written a book on the subject.

I'm ninety-eight years old, but I'm still able to be very active. I go to church every Sunday, bake bread on Thursdays, and sew potholders, aprons, and other useful items to give to people. I make comforters and quilts for underprivileged children, and I can fruit and vegetables. In the past, I have spent a lot of time volunteering at a home for handicapped children. I also sing with a group; we go to convalescent homes and other places in the community to perform.

One of the hardest things to endure in life is to lose a child. My daughter died of cancer when she was in her sixties, and it still makes me sad to think about it. She was such a wonderful person.

Someone asked me what I have planned for the future. I told them I have a second book I'm working on. I also want to keep doing the same things that I am doing now. I spoke at a meeting of a Community Coordinating Council a few months ago, and I was surprised to be honored with three different awards recognizing my volunteer work.

16

Concluding Thoughts

As I interviewed the mothers who shared with me for this book, I thought, *Why didn't I talk to these people when I was raising my children? They really have a lot to offer.* And truly they do. I did not report all of the information the mothers told me because some things were repetitious. However, even the fact that there *were* repetitions was informative, especially when some subjects kept recurring in *every* conversation. Since there seems to be such a general consensus that these subjects are important, I thought I should tell you which ones they are.

- Without exception, every mother talked about the importance of having a husband who is involved with the children and who helps with the housework. Good husbands are definitely important in the lives of working mothers.
- Adequate childcare is a must, according to the mothers. To be able to work and not worry about the children, mothers must know their children are being well cared for.

- Priorities should be made and kept, with the mothers agreeing that God is first, the family is second, and all other things follow after those two.
- Traditions are very important for the family to have. Many mothers believe each family should make their own and that the children should be actively involved in those traditions.
- Family trips seem to bond families together. Again, without exception, the mothers from all the different families talked about how important traveling together is. All different kinds of trips were mentioned—some very inexpensive—but the message these mothers had was that whatever it takes, mothers should find a way to involve the family in a vacation together.
- Being involved, and supporting each member of the family is crucial to the success of the children, as well as to the parents. Family members who work and play together and support each other seem to develop high self-esteem.

While mothers also mentioned many different things they considered important (I've tried to give you most of these on the preceding pages), the six items listed above were the ones each mother seemed to zero in on, time after time.

Before I wrote the last page of this book, I thought I should check with my own children, and see if I had given them any pearls of wisdom which we might want to include here. After talking to them, the general consensus was, "No, Mom, I can't seem to think of anything right now. Maybe I'll think of something for your next book." Being a mother can be a very humbling experience! But doesn't the Bible say something about a prophet being without honor in his own home? The writer must have had mothers in mind when he wrote that.

Without having pearls of wisdom of my own to conclude with, I will turn to a much better source, the Bible.

The Everyday Bible describes a working mother simply and beautifully. In Proverbs 31:10–31 we find:

> It is hard to find an excellent wife.
>> She is worth more than rubies.
>
> Her husband trusts her completely.
>> With her, he has everything he needs.
>
> She does him good and not harm
>> for as long as she lives.
>
> She looks for wool and linen.
>> She likes to work with her hands.
>
> She is like a trader's ship.
>> She goes far to get food.
>
> She gets up while it is still dark.
>> She prepares food for her family.
>> She also feeds her servant girls.
>
> She looks at a field and buys it.
>> With money she has earned, she plants a vineyard.
>
> She does her work with energy.
>> Her arms are strong.
>
> She makes sure that what she makes is good.
>> She works by her lamp late into the night.
>
> She makes thread with her hands
>> and weaves her own cloth.
>
> She welcomes the poor.
>> She helps the needy.
>
> She does not worry about her family when it snows.
>> They all have fine clothes to keep them warm.
>
> She makes coverings for her bed.
>> Her clothes are made of linen and other expensive material.
>
> Her husband is recognized at the city meetings.
>> He makes decisions as one of the leaders of the land.
>
> She makes linen clothes and sells them.
>> She provides belts to the merchants.
>
> She is strong and is respected by the people.
>> She looks forward to the future with joy.

She speaks wise words.
   And she teaches others to be kind.
She watches over her family.
   And she is always busy.
Her children bless her.
   Her husband also praises her.
He says, "There are many excellent wives,
   but you are better than all of them."
Charm can fool you, and beauty can trick you.
   But a woman who respects the Lord should be
     praised.
Give her the reward she has earned.
   She should be openly praised for what she has done.

Bibliography

Bodin, Jeanne and Bonnie Mitelman. *Mothers Who Work.* New York: Ballantine Books, 1983.

Dodson, Fitzhugh. *How To Single Parent.* New York: Harper & Row, 1987.

Garrison, Jayne. *The Christian Working Mother's Handbook.* Wheaton, Illinois: Tyndale House Publishers, 1986.

Greywolf, Elizabeth S. *The Single Mother's Handbook.* New York: Quill, 1984.

Harrison, Beppie. *The Shock of Motherhood.* New York: Charles Scribner's Sons, 1986.

Houtz, Elsa. *The Working Mother's Guide To Sanity.* Eugene, Oregon: Harvest House Publishers, 1989.

Hull, Karen. *The Mommy Book.* Grand Rapids, Michigan: Zondervan Publishing House, 1986.

Olds, Sally Wendkos. *The Working Parents' Survival Guide.* Rocklin, California: Prima Publishing and Communications, 1989.

Pruett, Kyle D. *The Nurturing Father.* New York: Warner Books, 1987.

Sanger, Sirgay and John Kelly. *The Woman Who Works, The Parent Who Cares.* New York: Harper & Row, 1987.

Scarr, Sandra. *Mother Care/Other Care.* New York: Basic Books, Inc., 1984.

Sedgwick, Carolyn. *When Mothers Must Work.* Springdale, Pennsylvania: Whitaker House, 1988.

Shreve, Anita. *Remaking Motherhood.* New York: Fawcett Columbine, 1987.

Sprankle, Judith K. *Working It Out.* New York: Walker and Company, 1986.

Wang, Bee-Lan C. and Richard J. Stellway. *Should You Be The Working Mom?* Elgin, Illinois: David C. Cook Publishing, 1987.

Whelchel, Mary. *The Christian Working Woman.* Old Tappan, New Jersey: Fleming H. Revell Company, 1986.